My Heart Has No Home

A JOURNAL OF GRIEF AND HEALING

Thank you, Sherry!

by John R. Worsley

John R Woy

This book details the author's personal experiences with and opinions about death, loss, and grief. The author is not a physician or a mental health care provider. Some content contained herein relates to physical and mental health issues, but is not intended to provide direction, advice, or suggestions to the reader, nor should it be used as a substitute for consultation with a licensed physician or mental health care practitioner.

My Heart Has No Home: A Journal of Grief and Healing
by John R. Worsley

Copyright © 2022 John R. Worsley

Published by Together Editing Press
Editing and design by Together Editing & Design
855 El Camino Real, Suite 13A-190, Palo Alto, CA 94301, United States
www.togetherediting.com

Library of Congress Control Number: 2022930195

ISBN-13: 978-1-939698-07-0

Printed in the United States of America

This book is typeset in Book Antiqua font.

Front and back cover photos by John R. Worsley

First Edition: May 2022
9 8 7 6 5 4 3 2 1

Μακάριοι οἱ πενθοῦντες, Ὅτι αὐτοὶ παρακληθήσονται.
Blessed are those who grieve, for they will be comforted.
Matthew 5:4

Μακάριοι οἱ κλαίοντες νῦν, Ὅτι γελάσετε.
Blessed are you who sob now, for you will laugh.
Luke 6:21

This book is dedicated to the dozens of friends and family on Facebook who supported and encouraged me not only as I began sharing my grief journey, but as I continued it month after month. You are why this book exists.

And of course, to my Amy, my love, my sweetie. You gave me more than I can ever quantify, but most of all, you gave me you.

.

CONTENTS

PREFACE

Despite appearances (or future marketing efforts), this is not, primarily, a book explaining death, grief, or loss—because I don't consider myself an expert in any of those topics. What I *am* an expert in is my own experience grieving the death and loss of my wife, Amy Katherine Worsley Heil, and that's what this book is about.

One meaningful factor in my decision to go ahead with this book is that Amy was a Quaker and an activist for peace: she worked every day to make a positive difference in the world. It would be a perfect tribute to turn the breathtaking, unimaginably agonizing experience of losing and grieving her into something that could help people. On a more visceral level, I just want something good to come out of the horrendous ill of her loss, and I'm drawn to the idea of us as a team one last time, working from each side of the grave.

Why Write This Book?

Amy and I met in college in 1989, and though we only shared our sophomore year, we did not forget each other. We lived our separate lives for the next 23 years, staying in touch occasionally, before reconnecting and marrying in 2012. On January 13, 2021, not quite eight years into our marriage, Amy died of alcoholic hepatitis, complicated by ... let's just say there's a list. I'd worried about her heavy drinking all along, and after a bout of alcoholic hepatitis four months earlier, the possibility of her drinking herself to death took on more weight. Still, neither of us actually expected it to happen any time soon. Her death was sudden, as she went from serious-yet-stable condition to dead in maybe 14 hours. The way it happened—complicated by a storm, medication, and incorrect information—gave us no real time together before she was abruptly gone.

As I sat wailing in Amy's hospital room that day, it struck me that we in the U.S. don't talk about death enough; there are plenty of books we can seek out and so forth, but in our lives we don't really talk about what it's like to lose someone. I wanted to do something to change that, so I started posting on Facebook about what I was going through. At first the posts were short and directionless, but the comments I received were encouraging, and I started saying more. I discussed my pain and my flaws as well Amy's, and how those interacted in our marriage; I shared the struggles and darkest thoughts I had in my relationship with her. I talked about specific ways grief was hitting me in the moment, as well as what I was learning and how I was healing. And throughout all of my posts, of course, my passionate love for her shone through. And along the way it turned into something of a blog.

Over time, many people found my posts meaningful, moving, inspiring—and went out of their way to tell me as much. A few months in, one friend said he could see a book version of my posts being useful to counselors, and I pondered that. At the time, I wasn't sure I really had anything significant to contribute to such oft-covered topics as death, grief, or loss, but the weight of such feedback grew. Later, I ran into a friend who teared up as she talked about how much my posts meant to her. Eventually, I concluded that if what I was sharing made such a difference among my 200-or-so active Facebook friends, then there might be a lot more people in the world who would find it helpful.

A Medical Saga

Amy experienced sepsis in November 2015, and it changed so much about her and our life that it comes up repeatedly in my grieving posts. Sepsis is a life-threatening reaction by the body to infection, typically originating in a particular organ or body part but causing such an extreme degree of infection that organs can start to shut down. My Facebook friends already knew about our life-changing experience of sepsis, and I didn't have to explain. For new readers, here's what happened, with enough detail to convey how traumatic the whole thing was for both of us.

Amy wasn't well when we got together. While her overall quality of life improved dramatically in the three years following, her lifelong struggle with chronic reflux/heartburn had been worsening, and she was concerned. Testing revealed the culprit to be the muscle that should be closing to separate her stomach from her esophagus. It was completely inactive—meaning her stomach acids were sloshing right up into her esophagus and irritating it. The level of chronic irritation she was experiencing could lead to cancer. After a year or more of being mostly doctor- and hospital-free, she was reluctant to submit herself to surgery. When she found out that surgery could be done to reconstruct the muscle without having to cut her open, she decided to go ahead. Using a newer technique, the surgeon would make five small holes in her abdominal wall and operate via those holes with thin, delicate instruments. The risk was much lower than traditional surgery.

The procedure seemed to go well on Monday, and for the first few days she was recovering well at home in Hood River, but by Friday she was in excruciating pain and felt increasingly bloated. I took her to our local hospital, where the ER quickly determined that her condition was too serious for them to treat, and she'd need to be transferred to a larger hospital. In fact, her condition was serious enough she had to be flown—an ambulance would've taken too long and jostled her body too much.

So she was whisked off by helicopter to Portland, where she spent eleven days in the ICU and nearly died. Her belly had to be cut open, partly to relieve the pressure and partly to find the source of the infection; no source was ever found. I slept in her ICU room with her the whole time.

She made it through. Her brain was addled—complete with hallucinations and paranoia—and she weighed over 100 pounds more than she had the day of surgery. (When your blood pressure gets too low, pumping you full of fluid is one of the primary solutions a doctor will resort to.) Most significantly, her belly had been cut open in the ICU (I'll never forget the moment her primary surgeon removed her dressing and showed me her guts as casually as he would a skin rash). Thus began a three-month inpatient recovery focused on enabling her to go home while her belly healed enough to be sewn back up. She had a tissue layer laid down over her organs, onto which skin from her thigh was grafted. I lived in the hospital with her for the first month, then slept at a friend's house nearby after that, but I was there with her almost every day. I became an amateur CNA (certified nursing assistant), and sometimes thought of things the doctors didn't.

Once the graft was fully established, she went home to continue her recovery, and six months later her belly finally got stitched back together. She never got all that weight off, and for someone who'd struggled with bulimia and anorexia her entire adult life, the emotional toll was high. So on top of PTSD from her service in the Air Force as an EMT, she now had medical PTSD. And of course, it all took a toll on me, though as the support person I never really let myself look at that—I had to be there for her.

Counseling

Neither my marriage to Amy nor the content of this book would ever have been possible without counseling. One recurring theme in comments on my Facebook posts was how brave I was to share so openly. The thing is, it wasn't difficult for me. I've long been a fairly open person, and I was lucky to come across a form of counseling in my mid-20s that worked for me. I did a lot of it for maybe sixteen years, until I left Portland for Amy, and it transformed me: I learned how to heal from emotional wounds and recover my inherent nature; how to counteract the ways I've been conditioned—as a man, White person, Protestant, and so on; how to listen actively and caringly to another person; and more. In the process, I shed a ton of fear, becoming more outgoing and assertive while also showing more of my real self. The upshot is, my trauma and feelings were familiar territory that I was used to talking about. It also feels like losing Amy cracked me open, eliminating the remaining vestiges of self-protection that might have kept me from sharing all that I did. All of which explains why I never hesitated to share what I wanted to.

How to Read This Book

The heart of what you're about to read are my original Facebook posts for the first six months after Amy died, unedited except for the following: minor typos I'd never have made if I weren't typing through tears; some images cropped to make more space for text; and references in [square brackets] to images we couldn't get permission to use.

As I looked back over what I'd written, I realized I wanted to provide additional context that I either couldn't or didn't include at the time. That content became this book's "Reflections" to many of the posts.

Since I wrote them later, I don't want the Reflections to detract from your experience of reading my original posts as a strong emotional narrative. Therefore, the Reflections are added sideways and in italics. That way, if you want to read the book twice, the first time without the Reflections, you can do so—or you can read the Reflections with their respective posts as you go, by turning the book sideways.

Lastly, the original posts and the Reflections each have occasional footnotes. Post footnotes are printed immediately underneath the text; Reflections footnotes appear sideways, underneath their "parent" text. A few pages have both.

January 13, 9:53 PM

I sat with Amy as she struggled to breathe.

I sat with her as she took her last breath.

I sat with her as her heart beat its last.

I sat with her as the nurses cleaned her and put her in a bag.

I sat with her until the transport guys took her away.

I am more afraid of NOT grieving than I am of grief.

Reflections: I think I wrote this as I sat in Amy's hospital room by myself, and I can still remember a kind of defiance I felt as I wrote that last line. But it doesn't sound right now; yes, it's true that I've wanted from the beginning to get as much of the pain out as I can, and I sobbed and wailed my way through each of the developments I list in this post. Looking back, I see another factor in my decision to stay in her hospital room until her body had been wheeled away: desperation to cling to anything pertaining to Amy. For example, three months later I cried when I discovered her bank had closed her account — and she was proud of her low account number, having acquired it decades ago. In retrospect I couldn't expect them to contact me because she'd never set that up, but it was a piece of her I wanted to control saying goodbye to. So it makes sense that I'd stay in that room as long as I could.

January 15, 9:20 AM

I'm sure you're all wondering what happened to Amy. She died of cascading organ failure triggered by alcoholic liver damage.

She'd hate me for telling you all that, but at this point I care about you more.

Please be honest with yourself about your relationship with alcohol, and be realistic about the fact that it can kill you quickly.

Amy had a bout of hepatitis in September, at which the doctor said her liver showed initial signs of damage. She cut down on drinking but didn't stop. Based on what that doctor said, when she started to get sick again, I just thought this was the point that I would be finally able to insist that she stop. For the first time she was honest with doctors about her drinking, and I was so hopeful. Then in less than a day, she went from very sick but stable to dead.

Alcohol doesn't fool around.

January 15, 6:28 PM

I have been unable to take an iota of pleasure in anything, even our beloved corgis (though I'm grateful for having them with me). And not even sure I'd want to take pleasure in anything since Amy's not here to share it with me.

But it occurred to me that, far from it being somehow inappropriate, Amy would want me to be happy – and more than that, embracing joy would actually be honoring her.

That is such a comforting thought.

Reflections: The house we had made our home was overwhelming to me at this point. Everything for 50 miles around reminded me of her absence because I left my life to join her in the Columbia River Gorge, where she'd already made a life for herself. "It's all you!" I would cry. The comforting thought is significant because it counters my first impulse, which is that to feel anything but pain without Amy is somehow a betrayal, that I can only honor her by staying miserable. So it's not enough to tell myself that Amy would want me to be happy; I need a message that's the opposite of what I'm feeling. "The best way to honor Amy is to embrace joy" does that, and I still need to remind myself of it periodically.

January 16, 9:39 PM

Amy's lap was a favorite corgi spot. I'm doing my best to fill in.

Reflections: In the photo, I'm sitting in Amy's recliner (which gets a later post[1]) since Amy basically lived there from 2016 onward. Prior to her death, I'd only sat in it once or twice because there were so few times when I was home and she wasn't. At this point in time, I sat there a lot simply because it was her bed, really, as well as her office, and that blanket was hers, and like I said, I just wanted everything Amy all the time. Amy and our dog Myra had a special relationship (also discussed in a later post[2]), so for Myra to want up on my lap while I was sitting in Amy's place ... I can still cry over that moment.

1 February 13, 9:35 PM
2 January 27, 6:56 PM

January 17, 6:57 AM

One of my favorite photos of Amy, capturing the playfulness I so adored.

Reflections: I have a dozen photos of Amy from this moment with our rescue dog Courage, but this is still my favorite of them. The way her hand is caressing him. The way she's making eye contact. The way her head is cocked. Then, of course, the way she's matching his lightly-panting tongue. But most of all, the way she so clearly loves him. It's all so very Amy, and captures the essence of what drew me to her. As the months pass, the pain of my loss comes up spontaneously less often, but at least once a day I look at this photo — now framed and hanging in the den — and cry for how I miss her.

January 17, 9:47 AM

We're all waiting for Amy to walk back in the room – surely she just went to the bathroom and is coming right back.

Reflections: This wasn't the first time the dogs had been home without Amy. Two of them had been boarded elsewhere for three months at one point. But to be here with me and not Amy was new for all of us. And while as a human I could understand what was going on in a way the dogs couldn't, the suddenness and circumstances of Amy's death were impossible to believe (I still feel like "what the hell?" about that). I have said, sobbed, and wailed "you can't be gone!" countless times. So the "I don't understand, where is she?" sense I got from the dogs in this moment was one I felt keenly.

January 17, 6:32 PM

Mornings are the worst, but the waves of despair are gradually waning, and my appetite is picking up, and my sleep is slowly improving. I'm taking care of myself. So if you're worried about me, that should encourage you.

Reflections: Despite being exhausted from hours of crying every day, sleep was elusive because it was hard to get my mind off the pain long enough to fall asleep; I'd lay down and try to empty my mind, but waves of pain would keep washing over me. I had to make myself eat despite having no appetite. But I did it because I knew running out of energy would make everything worse. I think I ate a lot of soup and energy bars, and after two or three days I resumed a bit of my exercise routine. The fact that a mere four days later, I was already thinking about everyone else enough to post this rather amazes me.

January 18, 8:07 AM

As a retired Air Force nurse, putting out our flag on designated days was important to Amy – she circled those days on our calendar.

Once upon a time she put it out herself, but for a while now she'd put it by the front door in the morning for me to put out. I had a good cry over the fact that she wasn't here to do that today.

Reflections: The fact that Amy stopped putting out the flag herself is part of a pattern we'll see in play repeatedly. The list of things she stopped doing, or did less frequently over time, is a long one, and one that I've had to grieve for on its own because I don't fully understand why it happened, and because it feels like I've been slowly losing her for years.

January 18, 3:47 PM

This was Amy's last Instagram post.[3] She put a lot of thought into her captions. This one was:

"Wait. Wuht? My pawrents totally forgot my barkday, and I will proceed to wreak havoc upon them! Bark out to my sibs!"

3 Her Instagram account name was Myra_and_Meatloaf_and_Merlin, and she posted mostly about our corgis; see also June 24, 9:00 AM.

Reflections: I think hidden behind this post is the fact that I was scouring the house and Amy's electronic devices for ... everything, anything, to do with her.

January 19, 8:50 AM

Amy was a Quaker, and her values reflected it. Here are some examples from around our home.

Reflections: It's no accident that "peace" is the most common theme here. Perhaps ironically, Amy's military service seems to have left her with a deep-rooted desire for peace in the world. Much of her political activism was dedicated to promoting peace. It was such a fundamental part of her that I'm crying right now just thinking about it.

January 19, 8:09 PM

Amy had a beautiful voice as a writer, but she shared so little of it with me. Despite that, I kept telling her the world needed her voice in it. Now that she can't stop me, I'm trying to find every scrap I can, with an eye toward publishing. Stay tuned...

Reflections: I suspect that while she aspired to "be a writer" in the official sense of getting her work published on some recurring basis, Amy'd given up in any serious way after years of rejection – an experience that certainly crushes many a writer. I wanted so fervently to help her overcome that. I also suspect that she refused to share what she was writing with me because she wasn't, in fact, writing much. She was used to feeling competent, and productive, and accomplished, and it breaks my heart to think that she might've been pretending to write more than she was, just to avoid feeling bad about herself. At any rate, I had the impression from the way she talked about her writing that I'd find a whole trove of recent pieces. I never did, though I found an older trove. As to my motivation for focusing on this topic six days after her death, I see now that it was part of a general desperation to cling to what was left of her. Even the desire to understand her better was a way of escaping from the overwhelming loss – there'd never be more Amy, but by understanding her more, I could feel like there was.

January 20, 7:25 AM

Since I am far from perfect, there is a lot more I could've done to show Amy I loved her. But I made a point of several things: I always said goodbye when I left the house (even in the middle of a fight, because you never know what'll happen), I always hugged her in the morning, and at bedtime I always told her I loved her and gave her a real kiss.

That last one became a sweet little game. Amy had a hard time believing she was lovable (which is heartbreaking since she so clearly was), and her most likely reply to "I love you" was a confused "Why?"

Eventually I hit on the idea of just repeating myself gently until she stopped questioning it. Being the playful person she was, she went along with the spirit of it, and I'm so glad we were able to find a way to short-circuit her resistance.

Reflections: Before this approach, I had a difficult time with her negative responses to "I love you." Her second-most-common reply was probably, "Someone has to." And it's true, I did have to. Not in a compulsory sense, but because given who I am and who she was, I was never not going to love her. I never said that, though; I wasn't sure how she would take it. I remember times when I attempted a serious answer to her "Why?", because she occasionally insisted I do so. I'd say something about the qualities I admired in her, or highlight something she'd said or done recently that exemplified her lovability. I think I did say something to the effect of "Because you're you" at least once. But I knew that while she could take some pleasure in the moment from those responses, they weren't really making a difference – which is what I always wanted to do. So this playful approach was my way of saying, "Just accept it," which is what she needed to do, and the fact that she went along with it meant so much to me.

January 20, 8:54 AM

I'm watching the inauguration ceremony[4] and mourning the fact that, after suffering so much from the events of the past four years, Amy didn't get to see this day. She would've sucked the marrow out of today.

4 The inauguration of President Joe Biden and Vice President Kamala Harris

Reflections: As a Quaker and a progressive political activist, Amy found the Trump presidency traumatic. And as someone who fundamentally valued being informed about the world, she put hours every day into reading and watching news – she didn't shy from it. It all took a toll on her. She drank more to cope with the pain, and repeatedly voiced the desire to leave the US. "This isn't my country," she'd say. And I'd think, "This isn't my Amy." For her – a veteran who was proud of her service to her country and an activist who worked for peace – to feel so overwhelmed that she wanted to flee rather than fight speaks to just how difficult it all was for her to deal with. She made it through, only to die with the January 6th attack on the Capitol hanging over Biden's inauguration. I can easily imagine her crying with relief and joy as she watched the peaceful transition of power that we weren't sure would happen.

January 21, 11:39 AM

My accomplishment for this morning was the last clothes Amy wore. They were in a hospital bag, carefully folded by her when she changed into her hospital garb.

That bag has been sitting on the dining room table where I dropped it when I got home. I knew that taking those clothes out was going to be huge, and I haven't been able to face it until now.

The clothes are in the washer, and I'll probably have another good sob when I have to put them away for the last time.

Reflections: There are plenty of things in our house that still sit just where they were when Amy last used them. Even without grief involved, I have a well-developed ability to ignore things sitting around the house – which conflicted with Amy's need for order. In my head, it's always about priorities, and with low-priority things, I'll get to them when more important things aren't pulling at me. That can be months, a year even. But a bag of clothes sitting on the dining room table was never going to be something I could ignore for long, because that table isn't a storage place. At worst (as it has been without Amy) the things sitting around on it represent a to-do list. I'll never be a slave to "what Amy would've wanted," but neither can I abandon all concern about what was important to her. I'm still trying to find that balance.

January 21, 4:57 PM

Season 2 of *Derry Girls* is slaying me – just within the first three episodes are two plot lines that remind me of Amy's high school stories: the school newspaper article plot and the 'sneak off to a concert' plot. She'd've enjoyed them so much.

Reflections: Oh, Amy's stories … she loved to tell stories from her life, and doing so gave her a distinct animation that not much else did. And since she'd had a full life, she had a lot of material to draw from. Like so much else, at the time I didn't fully appreciate them. Her stories were usually prompted by something in passing, so they often felt disconnected, like random leaves floating in a stream. As a result, I listened to them for enjoyment, but without the kind of attention I'd've needed in order to remember them better; I think I do that a lot with people. What I would give to be able to retell any of her stories! I remember the gist of some, but I can only imagine how many I've lost. Which, of course, feels like losing part of Amy. I kept gently pushing her to write them down and put together a memoir, and I think she was interested. It's easy to feel guilty. Horribly guilty, even, but the lesson here is, once again: Don't Take People for Granted. I want to strive to pay better attention to people talking about themselves and their lives.

January 21, 10:30 PM

It's possible that the most simple change I face is the most painful: how can "we" and "our" ever become merely "I" and "my"? As in, how can the home Amy and I created together ever be just my home?

Reflections: This is the first of several posts about my language struggles.[5] I have no idea how many other people run into this, since my brain is quite particular about language. There's a time-based element, in that people give you a pass for a while if you keep saying "we" or "our," and after a while it starts to feel awkward. Clearly I am part of "we," but the vast majority of what I now have, I'd never have had were it not for Amy. Saying "my house" feels like taking credit for something that she could rightfully claim the bulk of the credit for. I've also resorted to using "the house" to bridge the gap between the point after which it feels awkward to say "our house" and the still-to-come point at which I can handle saying "my house." I probably worry about it all too much, but to switch to "I," I have to fully accept that she's gone – and I'm not there yet.

January 22, 9:01 AM

This is one of my favorite photos of us, taken summer of 2013 at McMenamins' Edgefield Hotel.

Reflections: I don't know how fond of the Edgefield Amy was before we got together, but it quickly became our favorite place to stay. This is the only photo us there that I'm aware of, which makes it more precious. While Amy didn't like it, another photo I took of her on that bench has been my phone's lock screen image for the past eight years. Looking at this now, I see the relaxed affection that marked the good moments we had, and I can feel her hand on my leg and my arm around her.

January 22, 2:58 PM

In the aftermath of the horrible sepsis Amy had in 2015, she was never able to fit her wedding rings back on her finger. And she didn't want to get them refit, because of course the plan was always for her to recover her health and weight.

This is my great-grandmother's ring stand, and our rose gold rings were made in part from her tiny gold wedding ring.

Reflections: Amy had an eclectic collection (an eclection?) of rings already, but she mostly stopped wearing any rings from 2016 onward because she'd gained so much weight they didn't fit. The feeling of being out in public with her and being the only one of us wearing a ring never stopped being uncomfortable. That fall, despite having gained weight fairly steadily for several years, her fingers had somehow thinned enough that one day she showed off her finger with the wedding rings on it. Yet she still didn't start wearing them, and I didn't ask her why any more than I had ever pressured her to do something to resolve the situation. She was so insecure so much of the time, I think got used to just adapting to whatever she did rather than risk upsetting her by asking why. Not that a widow or widower's decision to stop wearing a wedding ring is ever easy, but all this history makes it even harder for me to imagine doing that.

January 23, 7:18 AM

My sleep is returning to normal, which is helping. I worked a bit yesterday, and it was exhausting, but I have to ramp up because my bereavement leave ends Tuesday.

This experience of grief hasn't followed any 'stages' – it's been a chaotic mix of denial, anger, and depression from the start. I still fundamentally can't believe she's gone and that I have to go on without her.

Reflections: And going on a year later, I still fundamentally can't believe she's gone and that I have to go on without her. Even with all the healing and re-evaluation I've done and the insights I've gained. As for bereavement leave, the startup I was working for didn't even have a bereavement policy, but thankfully they created one for me, and decided on two weeks. That first two weeks were the hardest, no question, and I don't know how anyone could go back to work before then — even three months later I struggled to do my job normally.

January 23, 3:10 PM

Five or six years ago I came across felt ornaments in a local store, got a few, and Amy liked them. So I've been getting more each year, and last year she declared she wanted an all-felt ornament tree, so we doubled down on them as gifts this Christmas to get her closer to that goal.

Next year we're planning an all-felt tree for Christmas, in Amy's honor.

January 23, 10:37 PM

I feel like I gave away a part of Amy today – B[6] now has all the Asian condiments, pastes, sauces, etc. that Amy loved to cook with, but which I am useless with. The empty spaces in the fridge will be painful, but I think Amy would love that these things are now taking care of B by feeding her.

---

6 Amy's daughter, Brooklyn

Reflections: Giving away parts of Amy turned into a choice I have continued. I've tried to find someone I know – or can at least meet – to give Amy's things to, rather than just dumping them at Goodwill. In part this gives me more opportunities to grieve and say goodbye, and in part it's meaningful to her friends and family to have little bits of her life, and in part it just feels appropriate for who Amy was – through her things she can keep making people's lives a little better.

January 24, 8:48 AM

Amy loved a good meme, and regularly watched *CBS Sunday Morning*. The inauguration Bernie meme would have brought her endless delight, and to see this... I can't imagine how she'd've eaten it up.

Reflections: I still laugh and cry at this. It's funny by itself for CBS Sunday Morning – which even when it goes for humor still feels very adult to me – to indulge in something as purely frivolous as this meme. And it's funny because it's so easy to imagine Amy laughing and enjoying it. She had a gift for recognizing meme-worthy moments, and it's quite possible she'd have jumped on the internet as soon as she saw Bernie in that chair wearing those mittens. And, of course, it's sad because I don't want to have to imagine Amy doing all that; I want to have seen her doing it.

January 24, 11:54 AM

Over a year ago, I started saying a nightly gratitude prayer, one major component of which (of course) was "thank you for another day with my Amy". Having to change that language focused me on the thousands of days we had together.

And that led me to another thought, which talking to Amy's sister Sara just now helped highlight... when we reconnected as adults and got together, Amy was seriously unwell both emotionally and physically. It's quite possible that she wouldn't have lived another eight years. The idea that my love for her gave her a longer and better life than she'd have had otherwise means more than I have words for (though I will always wish we had more time together).

Reflections: I'll never forget the moment that first night, when I got to this part of the prayer and realized I couldn't say "for another day" because that had been the last one. "My Amy" was how I often referred to her. I have a cousin named Amy, and several friends as well, but of course in my wife's presence confusion would've been rare, so I think my attachment to this phrase represents how grateful I was that after 20+ years of loving her, we were together in love.

January 25, 12:30 PM

One of the factors that makes Amy's death even more painful is that she was so gorked out on meds the day/night before that I didn't get to talk to her. We didn't get to say goodbye.

I've thought about calling the hospital to talk to her doctor and ask how much he thinks she was aware of what was happening. But Amy lived with anxiety and terror simmering just under the surface all the time, waiting to boil over, and the truth is that if she'd had any hint of what was coming, she might well not have been able to handle it. So maybe this was better for her.

Reflections: I'm rarely one to seek comforting thoughts just for their own sake, to avoid feeling something painful. So this was hardly the end of the subject for me, as you'll see in later posts.[7] It occurs to me as I write this that, in fact, it's selfish to want the manner of someone's death to be just the way I want it rather than the way they need it. Maybe I'm wrong and Amy would've surprised me with an ability to handle knowing she was dying, but the way it actually happened could easily be, in fact, a kind of mercy for her.

7 *February 20, 7:42 AM / June 3, 11:58 AM / June 11, 10:18 AM*

January 26, 12:20 PM

Today is a hard day. I'm tired of this Amy-less reality being my new
normal. And my bereavement leave ends today but I can only handle bits
of work here or there. My mind has great difficulty focusing on anything
complex for very long.

Reflections: The mental effect of this level of grief is one of the aspects of losing Amy that surprised me the most. It wasn't that I couldn't focus on anything or think about something. But the "higher" brain functions like analysis, connecting related information, and information tracking were extremely difficult and exhausting. And it wasn't just for work – playing games and cooking were just as challenging. It took easily four months for my mind to recover in this regard.

January 27, 6:56 PM

Myra is the corgi that started it all[8] in 2014. Corgis had been Amy's dream dog since childhood, and she randomly ran into Myra and her breeder in Hood River. Myra took to Amy within a few minutes – which her breeder said she'd never done before. So we got Amy her dream dog, and Amy often said Myra was a lot like her.

Myra is opinionated and a bit bossy. She is always alert for intruders (including those driving by a block away), patrols the yard and inspects everything. She hates being outside when all the humans are inside and whines at the nearest window so we know she's dying out there. She's a

---

8 We acquired three corgis over the years, and became bona fide corgi people, something all my Facebook friends know.

fighter too, and once she starts a fight she wants to finish it. She's also a squishy sweetheart who loves chin and ear scratches and playing fetch. Whenever we left the house without her, Amy would say, "Myra, you're in charge."

Reflections: Myra meant so much to Amy that she'd say, "Myra, you don't get to die, okay?" Between that and Amy comparing herself to Myra, you can imagine what Myra now represents to me. She's like Amy's avatar, and the thought of losing her is overwhelming.

January 28, 8:00 AM

A message in soot?

Reflections: See the collection of heart-shaped objects in the photo for January 19, 8:50 AM – the images and sayings posted around our house – for an illustration of specifically why this was meaningful.

January 28, 8:44 PM

Amy recorded *Close Encounters of the Third Kind* last spring, I think with the intent of watching it with B (every so often we'd make her watch a classic movie), but we never watched it at all. Amy was uncharacteristically not up for movies very often in recent months.

This movie never gets old for me. I fall for the creepy building sense of mystery every time.

Reflections: Regarding "uncharacteristically not up for movies," early in our marriage watching movies became one of our favorite things to do; it wasn't something I did a lot of before that. There were several years when we'd drive into Portland to just to watch movies all day that we couldn't see locally (boy, did I love that!). But somewhere along the way I developed a sense of urgency about it. Maybe it was the 300+ movies in my Netflix disk queue, I don't know. Amy largely controlled what we watched, so all I could do was say I'd love to watch a movie, and maybe we would. And if we didn't, I'd often sit there resenting whatever else it was she chose to watch, because it wasn't a movie. Thankfully, this fall I was able to re-evaluate a bit, to think about her needs more, and better accept her choices. In retrospect, I can see that the infrequency with which she was up for a movie back then had a lot to do with the adverse mental effects of the liver damage she was dealing with – and possibly the long-haul Covid she clearly suffered from, so I'm relieved I was able to make that adjustment.

January 30, 4:05 PM

Amy kept a list on the fridge of meals she was planning to make. Though I've hardly had to cook for eight years, I intend to make these meals for myself – and for our neighbor Bill, because Amy usually shared some of the meals she made with him; he's an old single guy, and a good neighbor who loves our corgis.

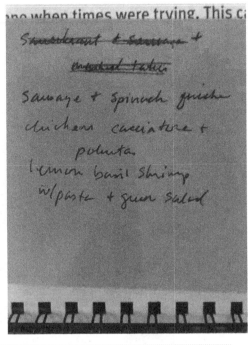

Reflections: I'll never forget the first time I walked into the kitchen after Amy died. As overwhelming as the rest of the house was, the kitchen was almost too much to bear since, more than anywhere else, it was "her place." Up until this point in my grieving process, I'd been relying mostly on a "meal brigade" that folks in town had organized, but that was winding down. So I had to start thinking about how I would feed myself. And a pattern was starting to emerge for me around this time: I was going to try to embrace things that had been important to Amy. To at least try them out. Wanting to honor her was certainly a major motivation, as was the fact that this approach would give me more opportunities to mourn what I miss about her. On another level, it's possible this was actually a way to postpone having to let go of those things – which I don't mean in a bad way. All along I've been giving myself the slack I needed to figure out when I'm ready to face letting go.

January 30, 9:43 PM

You might've seen my post a month ago about the 100 movies poster Amy gave me for Christmas, and how many I haven't seen (she was always amazed how many classic/well-regarded movies I haven't seen). She had recorded this one but we didn't get around to watching it.

So I watched it tonight, and I'm so curious what she thought of it. Though it's well done, I didn't get much out of it. But I plan to watch all the missing movies on the poster, just as we would've together.

January 31, 6:41 PM

I made a sausage and spinach quiche! It's light and moist, and a little bland, but good enough to eat.

And most importantly, I cooked for myself. I'm sure that's a big relief for Amy.

Reflections: The single most consistent way Amy took care of me, and Brooklyn, and even our neighbor Bill and others, was by making sure we were fed. Even during hospital stays, she'd worry about us eating, and ask friends or family to help make sure we had something to eat. So that's why I thought she'd be happy to see me cooking for myself. And as I mentioned, the mental coordination required to make this left me exhausted – I think I needed a nap.

January 31, 10:35 PM

I have been encouraged (thank you Juliana) to keep sharing my grief journey, so I will.

I started doing that because I figured we don't talk enough about the nitty gritty reality of it, and I wanted to do something to change that.

I also figure that what we each have to share, with ourselves or those around us or the world, is something no one else can share—and sharing what we can is enough. We don't have to worry about who it does or doesn't help.

Reflections: This is probably the point at which I realized I was doing a thing, that my offhand "we need to talk about death more" reaction posts had become an ongoing effort that people were finding meaningful. So I started sharing more of my thoughts about the grief and loss itself.

February 1, 7:59 AM

I got Amy last year's virtual Corgi Walk in the Pearl[9] calendar for Christmas AND paid for a photo of Merlin and Meatloaf to be included. This is the first month she won't see.

This highlights another element of grieving I hadn't thought about before: I haven't just lost Amy here in my life now – I've lost all the moments and experiences I thought we'd get to share for decades to come.

9 Corgi Walk in the Pearl is an annual fundraising event for the Oregon Humane Society; the "Pearl" is the Pearl District in Portland.

*Reflections: Boy does that understate what I
was feeling – losing the future I thought I had is
an enormous blow with all sorts of ramifications:
realizing how much of my identity was based on
what I expected the rest of my life to look like,
having to face a staggering array of choices I didn't
want to have to make because every one of them
would remind me that Amy's gone, and so on.*

February 1, 11:24 AM

This was Amy's first tweet, to me: "I love you".

Reflections: I still have this tweet open in a browser tab, and as I start my morning email–social media reading routine, I look at it so I can say "I love you too" in reply. I guess it stands in for the "I love you" she didn't get to say before she died. Plus, that little one-eyed critter she used for her Twitter profile is just so Amy.

February 2, 7:48 AM

This was Amy's last fridge magnet contribution, and it is so beautifully her.

Any single person's protest is inherently small. A protest movement is, ultimately, formed of individuals each doing their small protest – together.

Reflections: I may never take this down. Working to make the world a better place, from her recliner, with her laptop, through her browser, was Amy's primary occupation after the sepsis. These six words capture that so well – and no, the fact that "protest" is bolded is not intentional. It comes from a fridge magnet set of words themed for our alma mater, Reed College. But even so, having that word stand out adds an extra level of impact to the statement that is just perfect.

February 2, 12:34 PM

I've finally put away the last clothes Amy wore.[10] I mentioned before[11] that it took a while to take them out of the hospital bag and wash them. Then they sat in the dryer for days. Then they've been sitting folded on the dining room table, where I walked past them countless times every day, unable to face the next step.

But suddenly I was ready, today, to put them back in her drawers and on shelves. And in doing that I was overcome by the ways her clothing tells the story of our time together, from the t-shirts she was always getting to the clothes she couldn't fit into any more to how often these past few years she would ask me to bring something down to her, or toss something down the stairs for her – because she often didn't feel up for climbing our extra-steep stairs.

---

10 June 29, 11:12 AM
11 January 21, 11:39 AM

February 3, 9:09 AM

Amy and I had been planning to attend the Sundance Film Festival in 2016, but winter 2015-16 was her horrible sepsis and three-month hospital stay. With the festival being virtual this year, I got a pass for today, which is all-you-can-watch of the awards winners.

This is the first of many cultural events Amy and I would've enjoyed together. So today's challenge is to watch as many of these films as I can. It's theoretically possible I can fit in six...

Reflections: The full effect of the sepsis comes not just from the medical PTSD it left Amy with, or from the toll her post-hospital body took on her self-esteem, or any of the other consequences that came after it, but in contrast to the period before it. 2014 and 2015 were her best period physically. Attending Sundance was only one of a number of major travel plans we were considering because she felt up for it. To go from that to what her life was like afterward was a huge loss for her – and, of course, for me.

February 3, 2:53 PM

It's mostly little things now that get me sobbing. I just used the last tissue in Amy's tissue box, by the recliner she lived in these past five years, and that set me off. That sounds stupid when I write it down, but it's one of the changes I've been putting off till I felt ready.

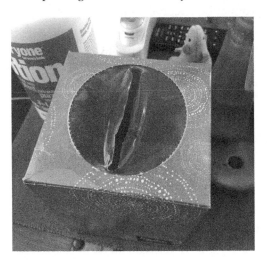

Reflections: "Mostly little things" represented a sea change from the near-constant state of grief I'd been through till then, crying on and off throughout the day from all the large-scale angles and levels to losing Amy. Put another way, I'd gone from crying "just because," to crying because something specific happened to trigger it. But looking back on it, I wouldn't count using the last tissue from Amy's tissue box as a little thing — it was something of hers, and the last tissue was a finality I knew would come, and had to prepare for. Little things now are much smaller and more incidental.

February 4, 9:38 AM

Addiction is a devious foe with an uncanny ability to convince the addict that they need – even deserve – the addictive thing. I certainly saw that at work in Amy. She knew she was an addict, and she knew what the end result could be, yet she also believed she had it figured out. She was gradually cutting down her alcohol intake, she kept it steady throughout the day, she drank a lot of water, she had a strong constitution, and she really thought she had a couple more decades to figure it out.

She was quite capable of quitting. She did, in fact, the week before she went to the ER. And just before we married, she quit morphine, Prozac, and Valium cold turkey at the same time because she didn't like the way they affected her ability to enjoy me.

I have faith in her love for me and B, and had she known where she was headed, I know she'd have chosen us over drinking.

But that's just not how it works. We don't get to know those things. We have to figure out how to do the right thing for ourselves and others based on an honest assessment of what's truly most important to us now. And that's hard to do.

Reflections: I remember writing "had she known where she was headed, I know she'd have chosen us over drinking," and how strongly I felt about it. Ironically, considering how I began this post, I think I was underestimating the power of her addiction. I know she'd have tried to choose us over drinking. But I'd have seen her justify and rationalize and defend her drinking for eight years, and I know those voices would never've stopped whispering in her ear. Her death was still raw for me at this point, and I was beset by all the what-ifs and could-have-beens. Even now, it's hard to let go of the thought that we were so close to a life in which she got healthy and strong.

February 4, 11:31 AM

Amy and I loved being at the Edgefield Hotel[12] for Valentine's Day, and we had a reservation. I've felt a strong pull to go anyway, but with the movie theater being closed, and with all the pandemic restrictions, I decided it doesn't make sense. So I canceled the reservation.

However... I don't suppose anyone wants to meet me there for dinner at the Power Station[13] on the 14th? (I'll pick you up if that would make the difference.) I'd love to honor the occasion anyway.

---

12 January 22, 9:01 AM

13 The Power Station pub is a restaurant on the McMenamins Edgefield Hotel property.

Reflections: I don't know why I said "I've felt a strong pull to go" – I was desperate to go. Desperate to cling to one of our favorite traditions – the pain of missing that experience lingered for months.

February 5, 8:54 AM

I thought I'd share this in case it's helpful or interesting. The thousands of hours of counseling I did when I lived in Portland gave me the foundation to deal the way I am with losing Amy. I learned two key things:

1) While all my feelings are valid, they aren't literally true. The best example right now is feeling "I can't do this – I can't go on in life without her." I'm crying as I type this because it feels so true. But it's not, and this knowledge enables me to feel the full intensity of every feeling, without worrying about it overwhelming me or destroying me or whatever.

2) In the context of #1, I learned that crying, screaming, and however else my grief manifests, are all healing things to do, that they let the feelings out of me. And however bottomless the well of grief may feel, as I let the feelings out of me, the well does in fact slowly empty.

Reflections: "In the context of #1" is the key. Believing that a feeling is literally true is like the cap on a bottle – as long as the cap is on, I can agitate the contents all I want, but nothing's coming out of the bottle. Only when I take the cap off can I start to empty the bottle. I really cannot overstate how much of a difference in my life these two concepts have made.

February 5, 2:05 PM

Amy loved Christmas. We'd been planning to take [the tree] down the weekend she went to the hospital, so it was all still up when I got home.

I decided almost right off that I'd leave it all up as long as the tree lasted. I thought it was doing fine until I finally noticed that, although it's still not dropping many needles, all the branches are drooping. And lo! it turns out the needles are all hard and crunchy.

So the tree will be coming down soon. My face needs to heal more first,[14] though, because I'll need to be able to bawl full-on for this.

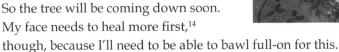

---

14 "My face needs to heal" refers to the fact that my dog bit me in the face a week before. I had stitches, and limiting the use of my facial muscles was key to the healing; clearly it's hard to emote much without facial expressions. This dog is a hunter and had found a dead bird to eat. In the heat of the moment, I forgot that raw bird bones are fine — it's the cooked ones that are dangerous for dogs — so I was doing everything I could think of to get him to drop it. He's also food-obsessed, and in a flash he jumped up and bit me. The incident was triggered by poor decisions on my part, and he's never shown any sign of aggressiveness toward people.

February 5, 4:06 PM

I've been collecting Amy's writing from various locations,[15] and found a letter from 2018 that she wrote to a reporter about his piece on the lingering effects of ICU stays.

There's a lot in it, but the part that got me was her saying she knew I'd never leave her, and that she feared she wouldn't be able to match my unconditional love. I know Sara[16] has been telling me Amy knew, but it sure helps to hear it from the source.

---

15   January 19, 8:09 PM

16   Amy's sister

Reflections: This is what she wrote: "I have a loving husband and best friend whom I have known since our sophomore year in college, and am sure will never abandon me. I wish I could bring the same level of confidence and unconditional love as he does to our relationship." Reading this was monumental! I imagine it would mean the world to anyone in my position. For me in particular, facing Amy's deep-rooted and seemingly intractable insecurity and low self-worth, my most fervent prayer in our marriage was that she be able to see God's love through me. This passage tells me I somehow succeeded, and I could cry for a month just about that.

February 6, 9:05 AM

In the course of watching CNN while I eat breakfast, I have cried at:

An ad for a women's hair loss reversal product, which reminded me how much I love Amy's hair and running my fingers through it.

A travel ad because it reminded me (I'd completely forgotten) that early on Amy and I were seriously talking about a trip around the world. I recall looking up the timing and cost of taking the Trans-Siberian railway.

February 7, 7:59 AM

Amy loved wind. We don't get much in winter – especially strong breezes like this – but summer can be epically windy.

The day we first reconnected in 2012 was a windy day. Amy had all the windows of her small corner apartment open for the wind to blow through. I think wind will forever be like an Amy avatar for me.

Wind blowing around a pine tree
https://youtu.be/fu7LE9_5mC0

February 7, 9:48 AM

I'm watching *CBS Sunday Morning* like Amy did,[17] and for their interview with Robin Wright they chose the *Princess Bride* scene with Wesley saying "death cannot stop true love," so of course I start sobbing.

It's not just for the obvious reason – Amy loved to talk about meeting Andre the Giant as a kid, and what a wonderful person he was.

---

17 January 24, 8:48 AM

Reflections: Many of my friends are as avid fans of The Princess Bride as I am, so this post assumes at least familiarity with the movie. I don't think I was thinking of this at the time, but there was a period when Amy called me "my sweet Worsley," playing off the fact that the hero's love interest calls him "my sweet Westley" at least once. This gives the movie special meaning to me now above and beyond the theme of true love.

February 7, 5:41 PM

The first two weekends after I lost Amy, it was really helpful to have NFL playoffs to watch – it was something to do, and something we'd have done anyway.

But somehow watching the Super Bowl without her is proving particularly hard.

February 7, 9:00 PM

To recover from my experience with the Super Bowl, I rewatched last year's Anya Taylor-Joy version of *Emma*.

And when Emma and Knightley kiss at the end, I had to cry, because Amy and I had a custom that when we watched a romance and the couple finally kiss for the first time, I'd lean over and kiss her – which I did when we watched this movie together.

Reflections: The magic of the first kiss is such a fundamental element of romance stories. I'll be watching a movie, knowing it's going to lead to The Kiss at some point, and knowing the heartbreak I'll feel not being able to kiss Amy. There's probably no way to avoid the pain, but I can say to her "I love you" instead of the kiss.

February 8, 9:02 AM

The grief is lightening. Not that I'm crying any less, but it doesn't feel so desperate and bleak as it once did.

Mornings are still the hardest. I cry before I even get out of bed, and again when I go downstairs knowing that Amy still won't be waiting for me in the recliner she had to sleep in (though she was usually awake because she had horrible insomnia).

Reflections: I find this post remarkable. It had been not quite four weeks, and I'd been so fortunate as to have only had to work a few days – meaning I'd been able to orient my life around the needs of my grieving process – and it took this long to notice the intensity of my feelings decreasing. Most people don't have the privilege of giving their grief that much time or attention. How hard must it be to go through this while having to work, or even work and parent?

February 9, 8:30 AM

As part of her need to feel like things were under control, Amy had a low tolerance for clutter (many a time I left something sitting out as a reminder, only to find it put away a couple hours later). So once a day or two, she would pick up all the dog toys and put them in the basket they lived in.

I haven't been doing that because I find it comforting to have them lying around – it makes the house feel a little less empty.

February 9, 4:00 PM

One of the hard parts of losing Amy so suddenly is all the items in our house that I never asked her about, or did ask but have forgotten the explanation. There could be great stories behind this painting or this ornament, but I have no idea.

On a larger scale, this factor is forcing me to look at the fact that inevitably, in the end, all our stuff moves on to other people, and in most cases all the meaning it held for us is lost.

I can imagine being okay with that, as our stuff goes on to hold new meaning for new people. But for now it's just painful because I don't want anything about Amy to be lost.

Reflections: Remember the desperation I mentioned, desperation to cling to anything Amy-related? "I don't want anything about Amy to be lost" is another facet of that recurring theme. It took me months to recognize this underlying truth and how it keeps me from letting go.

February 10, 10:25 AM

Here is one of the opinion pieces Amy wrote for the *Hood River News*.[18]
This particular one is especially poignant for me now, since it both honors
the greatest loss Amy had experienced, and was prompted by a random
encounter with an object.

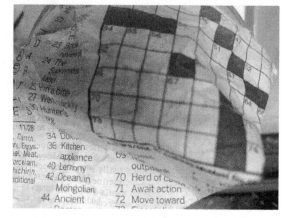

"Words matter: Clarity
found in Mom's crumpled
crossword"

---

18 *The Hood River News* was one of three local papers that were bought and
combined into the *Columbia Gorge News*. The full text of Amy's article can be found
in the appendix.

Reflections: I mention "prompted by a random encounter with an object" because those encounters play as much a role in my life now as in the life of anyone who's grieving. This post represents a new phase in which I start sharing about Amy herself. In part I wanted to honor her memory, and in part with this post in particular I wanted to share her beautiful writing voice. Looking back, I think on a deeper level I wanted to combat the sense of scarcity I felt. When a loved one dies, our experience with them becomes suddenly finite, bounded by a beginning and an end. All at once there's only so much of them. I couldn't actually create more Amyness, but by spreading her own expression of herself further out into the world, I could feel like there was more.

February 10, 8:52 PM

Amy and I enjoyed going for a drive, anywhere in this beautiful area. We were going to do that on New Year's Day, but she didn't feel up for it.

So I went for a drive today, up and around parts of Mosier Valley I hadn't seen before, then out Route 30 to The Dalles, returning on a back road. I've decided to call the Gorge "Amy Country" since it's all now indelibly associated with her.

It was good to get out and do something for myself. And of course, when I got home, I had to cry because I would so much rather have done it with her.

February 11, 7:32 AM

Amy was a survivor, a tough woman. She survived:

> Childhood (not everyone does)
> Deployment to multiple war zones
> A brutal husband
> Two divorces
> Three miscarriages
> Sexual assault
> A lifetime of eating disorder
> Massive sepsis that put her in the ICU

Knowing all that gave me compassion during the times she was less than the peaceful, loving person she wanted to be. It wasn't enough compassion to overcome my resentments and self-absorption, but it got me closer to showing the love I wanted to show her.

It says so much to me that, in the end, it was addiction that took her out, addiction that convinced her she had decades more to quit drinking before it killed her.

Reflections: I've since discovered references in letters to a second sexual assault, as well as ovarian cancer. I can't imagine what it must've been like for her to live through all that, to carry that much trauma around with her.

February 11, 1:30 PM

Putting away Christmas and taking out the tree was every bit as hard as I thought it'd be – but not in the way I expected. And I kind of hate Christmas at the moment.

I thought the act of removing the ornaments from the tree would be the worst part, but the worst is the gaping emptiness left in our living room, the stark visual representation of how my heart and my life feel.

I'm sure I'll get used to the empty living room – we always felt that loss when we de-Christmased. And I have the inducement of once again being able to watch movies on our projector with the sound system Amy got me.

Yet I can't imagine next November and December being anything but a protracted reminder of what I've lost. I will need a lot of support then too – I hope to God it's safe to gather by then.[19]

---

19 Due to the COVID-19 pandemic

Reflections: *It was an agonizing moment when I came back inside after dragging the tree out, and was hit by the vacancy it left. The tree stayed on the porch for another five months before I finally moved it to the back yard. But in that time, I've come a long way emotionally. As the next holiday season came along, I had to remind myself to cry more often, so the pain of Amy's absence didn't build up; at the same time, I was able to enjoy the moments that matter.*

February 12, 10:25 AM

Saying goodbye to Christmas Snoopy and putting him back in storage is a double whammy, because he doesn't just represent Amy's last Christmas, but also our shared love for *Peanuts* and Snoopy in particular.

Reflections: Amy not only loved to watch the classic Peanuts holiday specials, but she never tired of listening to the Broadway musical You're a Good Man, Charlie Brown. Snoopy was our favorite for his imagination and playfulness. By the following Christmas, the double whammy had dissipated, and Snoopy was the first Christmas decoration I wanted to get out.

February 12, 10:56 AM

Read what Amy wrote below, otherwise what I'm about to say won't make
as much sense.

This fits perfectly with my experience of Amy, as so many times I watched
her charm others in social situations,[20] then at home show me a staggering
insecurity and, at times, an ugliness of character that left me wondering
"which one is the real Amy?"[21] And at least for the past eight years,
putting on those social masks seemed almost always to require her to drink
a lot – which in turn tarnished my enjoyment of her social charm.

> A NEW DIRECTION – 1/92
>
> There is a place within me where all my masks are kept,
> And as the situation warrants I dig one out, dust it off, arrange it properly.
> Cheerful, intelligent, feminine, attractive, ambitious, embarrassed,
>   confident, demure.
> Each has its turn at the real world, and some are wearing thin.
>
> I'm tired of feeling like I have to force these out of me,
> Like if I didn't concentrate I would be devoid of character entirely.
> But if the creature hidden beneath the layers is frightened at the thought
> Of finding air and watching others run, turned off by ugliness and
>   insecurity.
>
> What I must do to protect myself has its sad side effects.
> No one knows me, and that hurts, but few have passed my test of honesty.
> Where it counts everyone suffers, but I have made suffering my life.
> Now I commit myself to a change of pace, a new direction, the masks
>   destroyed at last and a heart prepared to be real.

The truth is, I struggled enough with her behavior to me that my
measurement of what a good day was for us began with "no vexation",
and rarely went much higher. I'd even wonder sometimes if I'd made a
mistake in marrying her so quickly, that I should've gotten to know her
more deeply first. I can see now that a lot of that was just a matter of

---

20 March 15, 11:17 AM

21 June 4, 11:05 AM

perspective, of what I was choosing to focus on.

But I also had moments when it occurred to me to think that maybe – I don't know how much sense this will make to anyone else – her behavior was actually a sign of how deeply safe she felt with me, that she trusted my love for her enough that she didn't have to be "On" with me, and could show me the ugly.

And now this Voice of Amy Past reaches out to tell me I was right, and to vindicate my belief in redemptive love.

Reflections: Amy wrote this six months after finishing basic training, during her initial Air Force medical training. I don't know what prompted the self-evaluation, but clearly the new direction didn't stick. Or maybe it did at least in part, and the fact that she still wore masks so much of the time later in life is a testament to how much stronger they were in her youth. I think we all deserve someone in our lives who can handle the worst of our insecure, critical, angry, unreliable – whatever it is for each of us – sides. It is deeply meaningful to me that I got to be that person for Amy. And as the February 5, 4:06 PM post shows, clearly it was deeply meaningful to her as well.

February 13, 7:49 PM

And here is the last of the meals
Amy planned to make[22]: lemon
basil shrimp over pasta (I added
asparagus).

I'll probably leave her sticky note
on the fridge for a little longer
before saying a tearful goodbye to
it – and replacing it with my own,
starting with beef barley soup.

I think it'd mean a lot to her to
know that her meal planning
helped me get through this first
month.

_____

22 January 30, 4:05 PM

Reflections: I left her sticky note up for about five more months, and only then put my own up. Her sticky note I added to a pile of memorabilia. Cooking is such an ephemeral activity, leaving little behind it but memories, yet it feels odd that something so meaningful to her should be so little represented in the artifacts of her life.

February 13, 9:35 PM

Soooo hard to believe it's been a month since Amy died. In all the grieving I've done, I've barely been able to look at the fact that I watched her go. And it's still excruciating to me that I wasn't there for most of her last two days – after years of being there for her every day.

This is the recliner Amy lived and slept in for most of the last five years.[23] I just replaced the blanket she kept draped over the back (for pulling over her shoulders when cold) with this quilt the hospital gave me when she died. I call it her Death Shroud because that amuses me, and I'll take amusement where I can get it these days. I think she'd enjoy the name too.

23 February 14, 10:01 PM

Reflections: This might be the first real change I made related to Amy's life in this house. I think it stemmed from trying to figure out what to do with the hospital quilt, which is unusual in being an item with Amy-related significance that was never part of her life. I couldn't bring myself to just stick it in a closet or a box somewhere. Deciding to call it her Death Shroud made a real difference, in lending it some levity I know she'd appreciate (though undoubtedly it seems morbid to some).

February 14, 11:06 AM

Amy loved flowers, and I got into the habit early on of making sure there were always flowers in the house. While it didn't make sense to get the kind of big fancy bouquet I'd normally have gotten her for today, I did get something special.

Valentine's Day wasn't a big deal for Amy, something that took me a while to catch on to. A couple years ago, her response to the card I gave her was "aw, every day is Valentine's Day with you." It was a sweet thing to say, though at the time it felt bittersweet since so much of her daily behavior seemed to belie it.

But in keeping with my recent reevaluations, I choose to believe it now, and to think that her inability to show me its truth regularly reflects the overwhelming amount of emotional and physical trauma she lived with – rather than some defect in her love for me.

February 14, 3:59 PM

At one point, Amy was in the hospital on Valentine's Day, so I tried to decorate her room to reflect it, including these hearts. I brought these two back and stuck them in the den, one in front of her and one to the side, where they stayed to this day.

Before Amy, I'd encountered the idea that love is an action rather than a feeling, but our marriage is where I discovered the truth of that. We had a lot of fights over the years, and there were plenty of days when it felt like she hated me, and I was hurt and angry in turn.

But I always clawed my way back to the fact that I adored her and cared about her and wanted her. I apologized as often as I could do so genuinely. I did everything I could to stay civil.

It would've been easy to give up, to conclude that marrying her was a mistake – and those thoughts did cross my mind. But I chose to love, I chose to forgive, and I chose compassion. And I'd do it all over in a heartbeat... pain, anger, and all.

Reflections: I can't claim any particular virtue in the degree to which I stayed civil. It became quickly clear that responding in kind when Amy lashed out only made things worse, but that's hardly the reason I was able to restrain myself. Rather, in reaction to physical abuse as a toddler, I resolved that I would never knowingly do anything to hurt another person. The rest of what I describe being able to do, I ascribe to copious counseling.

February 14, 10:01 PM

Amy got this decal transfer when we bought this house, quoting a song from *The Nightmare Before Christmas*. I put it on a closet door in our bedroom, and at that point she was able to sleep in our bed at least some of the time.

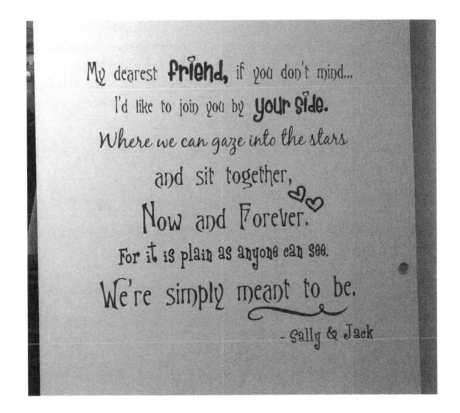

> My dearest **friend,** if you don't mind...
> I'd like to join you by **your side.**
> Where we can gaze into the stars
> and sit together,
> Now and Forever.
> For it is plain as anyone can see.
> We're simply meant to be.
> — Sally & Jack

But for these past few years, our flat bed was too uncomfortable for her, so I was the only one going to sleep to, and waking up to, this message.[24]

Early on when we reconnected as adults, she repeatedly expressed feeling like it meant something, so this quote fit at the time.

But the truth is that over the years, I saw fewer and fewer identifiable signs

---

24 March 9, 6:50 PM

of her love, fewer signs of affection, and I came to feel like this quote was bitterly mocking me. I hated it, honestly.

What a difference perspective makes. I see more clearly now that the change in her I was feeling wasn't about me – it's like Amy was contracting all over as a person, the cumulative toll of her medical traumas, and her drinking, robbing her of herself.

And the truth is that now I kind of do believe that our marriage meant something above and beyond. It gave her a new phase of life that probably extended her life and certainly gave her a lot more live for. And in that time, Amy made a difference in a lot of lives. My presence, and our relationship, made an enormous difference in B's life. I also feel like there's a way Amy will continue to live on in and through me... more on that later.

Reflections: Even without ascribing it all to Fate or God's Plan, when I look at the sequence of events that started with me trying to reconnect with Amy, and I look at who I was and who she was, I can't see it going any way but how it did. It's like human math: I'm going to make certain choices, of my own free will, and she's going to make certain choices, also of her own free will, and when you add those choices together, you're going to get our life together. I'm fairly attached to the truth and am not eager to console myself simply to feel better. But the more time I've had to look at the way our time together went, the more I do see meaning in it. As for the idea of Amy living on in and through me, I never posted whatever it was I was thinking, nor do I recall what it was. Yet this book, if nothing else, will certainly achieve that. Meanwhile, this quote also serves as the perfect reminder of how much time and energy I wasted on resentment and bitterness, something I'm determined never to do again.

February 15, 11:49 AM

After a month, I still fundamentally can't believe Amy's gone for good, that this is real, that it's not a nightmare I'm going to wake up from, that I have to keep facing thing after thing because she won't ever be here again – my most common wail is, "oh Amy, how can you be gone?"

It's still too much, and I still can't really imagine ever feeling any different.

Reflections: Almost a year later, that particular feeling doesn't surface as often now, but the agony of it – "How can you be gone?" – is alive and well. I've long had a strong feeling that death is just wrong somehow, and the sudden and unpredictable nature of Amy's makes that worse.

February 16, 10:33 AM

I've been diligently reading each day's
page in this book (thank you Lisa and
Kevin!), and today's entry talks about
how the world keeps on going around
us while we grieve.

I started bawling when I read this:
"Somehow we feel the earth should stop
spinning and acknowledge our grief."
But it's not about me – I don't need the
whole world to acknowledge my grief.
I want the earth to stop spinning and
acknowledge that Amy is gone.

*Reflections: The inexorable way life just keeps going
when we die can feel cruel in the throes of loss, but
imagine how easy it would be to never let go if life did
stop. If, as I'm coming to see, letting go is the beating
heart of healing from tragedy, then life's steady
march keeps that heart beating.*

February 16, 9:42 PM

Amy was an avid reader of *The New Yorker*, and it was the only place she ever submitted her writing to (she did eventually let me submit one thing elsewhere for her). She used to read whole articles to me, and we all used to flip through to read the cartoons.

She also frequently pushed me to inform myself better about what's going on in the world.

So today I opened one, to see if I had the attention to read articles. And I do, which is a good sign. I can't read them seriously at the moment, with any intent to ponder or remember the content – which is fine. My plan is to read all the remaining issues[25] until her subscription expires in June. Maybe I'll come to enjoy it and want to continue.[26]

What jumps out at me initially from this issue is how much NYC-specific content there is. Amy often talked about how much she wanted to go back there, and about how she'd go into the city during her first year at Bard College. So I'm sure she read every review of every NYC restaurant and performance and so on, and knowing that makes me feel closer to her.

---

25 March 14, 11:50 AM / April 17, 9:07 AM

26 June 2, 11:34 AM / June 25, 9:00 AM

February 17, 9:07 AM

The first random sobfest of the day was brought to you by this, which just happened when I set the bowl down.

Have I mentioned how desperately I miss Amy's playfulness,[27] miss the woman who once took turns with me spelling out words with the fingerling potatoes from our first harvest, who carried googly eyes in her purse just in case, who would arrange the fruit in the fruit bowl to make a face? That is the stuff of life for my spirit.

---

27 January 17, 6:57 AM / January 20, 7:25 AM

....

Reflections: In the throes of our occasional fights, or during bouts of resentment, I'd sometimes wonder if I was getting enough of what I needed in our relationship. I knew I loved Amy's playfulness, but it wasn't until I lost her that I could see how it met an actual need for me.

February 17, 7:17 PM

I happened to drive by the Providence Hood River hospital today, and started crying out of happiness that Amy would never have to go there again, or feel any of the pain, nausea, heartburn, anxiety, self-loathing, etc. that made life hard for her.

But it gets confusing, because that feels like an argument that it's better she died – which I don't believe. I know she was getting more than enough out of life to make it all worthwhile and planned to continue enjoying life as much as she could. On the other hand, then it can feel like I'm saying I'd rather she were here and suffering.

Being a word geek, I can solve this problem with three words: "at least now". At least now Amy won't ever have to... It's like a consolation prize – a wonderful, joyful consolation prize.

February 18, 11:10 AM

Amy was a Billy Joel fan, and if there were one song we considered Our Song, it was probably "You're My Home". The song ends like this:

> Long as I have you by my side
> There's a roof above and good walls all around
> You're my castle, you're my cabin and my instant pleasure dome
> I need you in my house 'cause you're my home
> You're my home

Even before she first played the song for me, back when I was commuting to Portland for work some of the time, I told her that it wasn't when I got off the highway that I was home, and it wasn't when I pulled onto our street, and it wasn't when I parked the car, and it wasn't when I walked in the door – only when I reached her arms was I home. She played it a lot when we drove to and from Portland, and so often she'd put her hand on my leg or my arm, or the back of my neck.

So this song really did capture truth for me. And now my heart is homeless.[28]

---

28 March 20, 9:40 PM

Reflections: Here is the genesis of this book's title. I had defined Amy as my home, and now she was gone. I lived in a place I had moved to just to be with her, and for fifty miles around the only reason I knew the area was her. It was overwhelming.

February 18, 9:48 PM

I just watched episode 5 of *WandaVision* – I think even Amy would've enjoyed this show, and she didn't like superhero-based stories – and now that I know (at least basically) what's going on, I so feel for Wanda.[29]

If I could do what she's doing, part of me sure would want to.

---

29   March 6, 4:31 PM

Reflections: For those who haven't watched the Marvel series, Wanda has sorcerous powers strong enough that she brings her dead lover back to life and remakes an entire town so she can have a life with him like they planned to, and raise a family. In the process, she mind-controls all the town's inhabitants to force them to go along with her scheme. It's a monstrous thing to do to a couple thousand people, but as someone in the throes of the same anguish the character was feeling, I could sympathize at least with the desire that led her to do it.

February 19, 1:47 PM

It has occurred to me to take videos of our house, because over time I'm likely to make changes (I've already made some minor ones), and I want to remember what it was like when Amy was here.

Reflections: I am ever so thankful I did this, especially with my crappy memory. Some people undoubtedly would have the state of their house at the time of their loss engraved in their mind forever, but not me.

February 20, 7:42 AM

The sequence of events leading up to Amy's death is still agonizing for me. I don't think I've told the whole story here.

I took her to the ER in Hood River on Sunday, and she was transferred to Portland that evening. I visited her on Monday, and she was mostly gorked out due to the Benadryl she so often got for nausea. We both thought this was just another hospital stay and that she'd recover.

One of her doctors or nurses said she'd be eligible for a liver transplant, so while I knew her case could be serious, I thought there was a path forward either way. So I went home, having told Amy I wouldn't be visiting the next day because it wouldn't be safe to drive in the huge storm we were going to get.

Tuesday I called her a couple times but wasn't surprised she didn't answer. I was more surprised she didn't respond at all by text. Late that evening a doctor called, and that's when I learned she couldn't get a liver transplant because she hadn't been sober, so now I knew the danger she was in. For some reason I still didn't call the hospital to talk to her like I'd done before when she wasn't answering her own phone.

And then Wed. morning as I got ready to go, the doctor called again to say she was dying and all they could do was switch her to comfort care. Even then I thought we had more time, so it was a horrible shock to walk in the room and see that she was struggling to breathe and non-responsive to my voice or touch.[30]

It was all a terrible conspiracy of events and conditions that kept us from having a moment to say goodbye or anything, and it's so painful to have to live with the fact that that's how it happened.[31]

---

30 June 3, 11:58 AM
31 June 11, 10:18 AM

February 20, 1:35 PM

Amy and I had been watching [NBC's musical show *Zoey's Extraordinary Playlist*][32] and loving it. While I had to wait several weeks to pick it up again because it was too close to home, now something about the way it deals with loss and grief is proving to be perfect for me.[33]

---

32 [Describes an image I couldn't get permission to include here.]

33 April 29, 2:01 PM

Reflections: *At the end of the first season, Zoey loses her dad, who has been deteriorating for a while. By "perfect for me," I meant that what she and her family go through in grieving him felt spot-on to me. It was helpful to see their grief treated with compassion, and to see it continue to affect them — to be given all the time it takes, rather than just highlighted here or there.*

February 20, 6:11 PM

I got my hair cut today. Amy had distinct opinions about clothing and style, and as she was fond of saying, "I have to look at you," but she seemed happy with the way I was getting my hair cut. She liked the little curls I get on the sides in back, behind my ears, when my hair's long enough.

In a poignant quirk of timing, the stylist I've been seeing since I moved out here retired last month, meaning I had to find a new one – and Amy had switched to our local stylist. So I went to her, and it was good to get to talk to her about Amy.

But I still sobbed on the way home, knowing that Amy wouldn't be waiting to see the results, and that in fact I could've done anything I wanted with my hair because she's not here to care — or to play with those little curls when they come back.

February 20, 9:19 PM

I've been waiting since last fall to see [Searchlight Pictures' film *Nomadland*], and it was worth the wait. I think Amy would think as highly of it as I do.

There's so much I could share, but I'll focus on this: I've wondered for years if I'm focusing too much on the future I want at the expense of the present. I struggled with that before Amy but even more with her.

This movie forced me to look at it this way: I want to live my life such that if I were to die today, I'd be pleased with my life so far.

And the truth is that I have. I got to make an incalculable difference not just in Amy's life but in Brooklyn's too. Whatever else my future may bring, that has made being alive worthwhile.

Reflections: Nomadland is a multiple-Oscar-winning movie that mostly takes place among a mobile community of people who have chosen to live in vans, RVs, etc. For me, it did a beautiful job questioning what makes life worthwhile. I have never planned for retirement, and that didn't change with Amy. What did change was how I thought about my screenwriting, which came to seem like our best bet at providing for our old age. Yet with a day job, I had to fit writing into the corners of my life, and all those corners were ones Amy wanted. It was like she "let me" write, in the sense that I knew she would rather I spent all that time with her, but she put up with me going to the office and, as she occasionally put it, "doing whatever you do up there." After her first bout of alcoholic hepatitis in September, I decided to prioritize her more, and let go of the writing I often did in the hour or so before bedtime. I'd check in with her, or just read her mood, and either go write, or not. I am now, of course, relieved beyond measure that I made that choice. But the larger point still remains, because for so long now I've been ordering my life around what I want the future to be, and sacrificing a lot in the present — when the present is actually the only moment we ever have. I don't know what the solution is, but being aware of it is the first step.

February 21, 10:01 AM

I grew up listening to NPR, but Amy put her indelible stamp on what I associate it with. She kept NPR on the radio 24x7 so the house would feel fuller, but there were also the idiosyncratic things, chief of which was how she'd sing the *Weekend Edition* theme as Beaker: mee mee-mee-mee mee mee mee-mee mee...

At least, she used to do that. It's possible a couple years have passed since I heard it – one more marker of the accumulated toll her physical and emotional trauma was taking on her.

From here on I think hearing NPR radio will be kind of like having Amy with me.

Reflections: I still can't imagine ever reaching the point of turning the radio off. Amy had the habit of turning it up when she was cooking (the radio is in the kitchen), then leaving the volume up, which annoyed me. I felt like it was yelling at me, and would turn it down when she wasn't there. I'd have been happy if one day she turned it off and left it off except when she was actively listening. So I'm surprised to find myself content to leave NPR on all the time, and to keep the volume at a level I can easily hear. I think it just goes with the kitchen experience, which still often makes me think of her. And when Weekend Edition's theme plays, I sing it as Beaker from the Muppets – which as often as not makes me cry.

February 22, 8:24 AM

As anyone who has lost a loved one knows, grief is a variable, complex process. But the loss itself can be layered, and each of those layers has to be grieved. Only this morning was I able for the first time to grieve the moment I learned Amy was dying, to revisit the incomprehensible shock I felt.

Here are some of the layers to my loss:

> Losing my hope that Amy would finally be able to kick her alcohol habit.
> Learning that she might not survive.
> Learning that she was dying.
> Realizing that she wouldn't get to say goodbye.
> Seeing her take her last breath.
> Walking into our house and being hit by the enormity of how empty my world felt.
> Realizing that I'd lost an entire future.

Reflections: Enough time has passed that I'm grateful I posted this list. I felt every one of those keenly at the time, and have grieved each of them to differing degrees, but at this point it all boils down to letting go. I like having this reminder of where I was then.

February 22, 2:47 PM

Amy kept very little email, presumably as part of her need for everything to be tidy. As someone who has (the text of, anyway) emails as far back as 1996, I always found that incomprehensible. She would even delete order confirmation emails before the order arrived, with the result that if the order was delayed, she didn't have a tracking number to look up.

But the one place she didn't clean up after herself is her Sent folder, so I looked to see how far back it goes – 2011.

In the process, I found a series of emails between her and her former pastor, that show a meaningful friendship she lost because he reached the point of insisting she join AA – and she wouldn't. All she ever told me of the people from that church was that they all chose her ex-husband over her. Oh Amy... my heart breaks for you.

Reflections: I was desperate to find every scrap of anything of hers. I pulled out all her tubs and boxes from previous phases of her life, I looked all over her hard drive, through her web browser history – everywhere I could think of. I've copied and saved all her text messages. One of the agonizing things about losing someone is the way our experience of them just stops so abruptly. I think I was trying to work around it by learning everything I could about her. And every time I found something like this email exchange, that illustrated her struggles, it hurt so much to think about how she'd been suffering; I regretted having been unable to help her more.

February 22, 9:24 PM

[The 2019 anime movie *Weathering With You*] was on my list of movies to watch with Amy. We wanted to see it when it came out, but B went to see it without us and we never went ourselves.

I'm noticing in a way I haven't before how common it is for characters in stories to have lost a loved one, and of course it's hitting me harder now.

Toward the end of this story, the boy is desperate to try to get to the girl, who's (essentially) been taken to another world, but people keep getting in his way. His anger boils over and he yells, "I just want to see her again" – so of course, I lost it.

Where's *my* portal on the roof of a tall building that takes me to Amy?

Reflections: The point in the movie at which the boy yells that line, he's trying to get to the roof of a building to go through a portal that would take him to her. As with my post about WandaVision,[34] I felt the character's pain keenly. I can still cry at the appeal of just stepping through a portal and being with Amy, but I've processed and healed enough since then that I'm coming to accept my continuing life and the difference I can yet make in the lives of the people who are still with me.

34 *February 18, 9:48 PM*

February 23, 12:06 PM

I realized this morning that I've been in denial about the fact that Amy's funeral service (for family) is this Friday. Her urn will be placed in a spot in a columbarium (wall) at Willamette National Cemetery.

I know she wanted to be buried there. I don't remember anything she said about casket vs. cremation, but since there's an eco-friendly dissolution process now, I thought she'd want it. And in keeping with her value on simplicity, I thought an urn would be better anyway. See the photo below.

Amy Katherine Worsley Heil

1970 - January 13, 2021

And now these three remain:
faith, hope, and love.
But the greatest of these is love.
— 1 Corinthians 13:13

Sadly, I've forgotten the several different things she said over the years that she wanted as her epitaph. As I recall, they were mostly things that amused her, not that would necessarily be meaningful to anyone else. I would, of course, have rather used one of those since it would've been specific to her. But although generic, this verse from the New Testament came readily to mind as representing her well enough.

And, of course, a corgi. If I'd had the attention, I'd have tried to find a suitable photo of Myra to use, but I didn't. So this is just a stock image.

Reflections: This was well over a month after Amy died, and it was still difficult to face her funeral service. I'd been working with friends on what to do for the service — and even that I could barely think about — but I was blocking out that the service itself was getting closer and closer. I see people who have burial services three days after their loved one's death, and I don't know how anyone does that. I think it would've been traumatic for me, would've prevented so much grieving I got to do. But I understand that people who want or need to bury the body have practical limits on how long they can wait, whereas this new dissolution process takes longer.

February 24, 6:15 PM

It has been a curious last two days, but I'm feeling lighter. Yesterday morning, I'd just finished sobbing about how painful it was to face Amy's funeral service coming up on Friday, when...

There are a lot of voices in my head, which makes it hard to take any of them seriously much of the time. But yesterday morning one of them started sounding like Amy. Not just speaking as though her – it had her sense of humor. It was trying to reassure me, and said, "It's not so bad being dead," which made me laugh. So whatever this voice is, I'll call it Amy. It's close enough.

Today I was struggling once again with the idea that now there's a lot more I can do in my life. That always leads me smack into the fear of going anywhere near anything that sounds like saying it's better that Amy's dead. But on the other hand, she's not coming back. Then it occurred to me once again that a language solution might work: start these kind of thoughts with "Since Amy's not coming back..." To which Amy replied by singing (if you're not familiar with the Monty Python song this is based on, trust me that this is funny):

"Always look on the bright side of death." [whistles tune]

Boy did that give me a good laugh, and it is so Amy. Just the kind of unexpected humor she sometimes tossed out, that made me overflow with love for her. So I've added a few more lines:

"Our life was pretty great,
We got about eight
Years of love and fun and musicals."

Reflections: This is a reference to the final scene of the satirical movie The Life of Brian *from the same guys who did Monty Python's Flying Circus. The actual line is "always look on the bright side of life." The idea of looking on the bright side of death is something I wasn't ready for until it popped into my head. If someone had suggested that a week or two earlier, it wouldn't have been helpful. But by this point, it was perfect, and I still laugh at it now. Because it's true – the only choice I have is what to do with my life now without Amy. As I become ready for it, why not look for a bright side?*

February 25, 10:20 PM

Today felt weird because it felt almost normal. I didn't cry much, in part because I was distracted by electronics deliveries and setting those up, and in part because I've been feeling lighter since the advent of "Always look on the bright side of death" per my last post.

To be clear, the meaning for me in that line is not literal. I've seen people cling to positivity because facing the pain of loss is too much, and that is not my path. I had to go through every day of the past month and a half of heavy grief to get to the point that I could find this line funny.

The meaning for me is contextual, part of feeling like Amy's telling me that it really is all okay. That she's okay. That she's not missing out on the things I want to share with her. That she forgives me for the ways I fell short of what we both wanted me to be. That I did the important things just right. And so on.

So for the moment, my dominant feeling when I do grieve is simply, "I miss you." Even if she's with me in spirit, it's not the same, and for me that difference is huge.

Reflections: I still find useful the thought that Amy says it really all is okay. It does wonders when I start to go down the Rabbit Hole of Regret, thinking "I wish I'd..." or "I'm sorry I didn't..." And it's also still true that the simple "I miss you" is usually the most truthful way to look at what I feel. I am, however, surprised to see that I'd reached this point so early — it feels like a later development. Or maybe the time that passed up to this point felt just as long as all the time since.

February 26, 9:51 PM

Well, Amy's hybrid Air Force/Quaker funeral service was today. I am eternally grateful to Judy and Johan and Sara[35] for supporting me in figuring out how to honor Amy, especially considering how hard it was for me to think about.

The key was realizing that to do her justice we had to honor her irreverent sense of humor, so I read two humor pieces Amy wrote when she was younger.

But Sara capped it all off perfectly by handing out packets of googly eyes to everyone, and the cemetery representative offered to put one in with the urn before they seal it up.

So I think it went well.

---

35 Amy's sister

Reflections: Reading those two humor pieces of Amy's certainly made me – and others – smile. What actually made Sara's contribution so much more perfect was the fact that the packets were actually labelled "Wiggle Eyes." I don't know if "googly eyes" is somehow trademarked? Or if it's just a bad translation? But I do know I busted out laughing – cackling, really – when I saw the label. And that was the best tribute.

February 27, 10:29 PM

My poor attention has taken a toll this past month.

I left a burn mark on a cutting board when I set a pot down on it straight from the stovetop.

I got Amy's favorite trivet a bit moldy by overwatering the poinsettia I didn't want to get rid of. This was hard to deal with because I can imagine how upset she'd have been.

And now I may have missed submitting the inscription form for Amy's urn spot on time.

I know what you're all going to say, and I've never been much of a regrets person, but in this already agonizing context, it's really hard not to feel bad about these things. It just feels like I'm not doing right by her.

Reflections: The feeling of not doing right by Amy covers a lot of territory. I've struggled to figure out what that's really about. It's easy to describe it as being devoted to her, but that's just a superficial description. The fact that I can't put my finger on it makes me suspect it comes from my early years of life. Whatever it is, it could well be the single biggest motivation I've had – not just since her death, but since the start of our relationship.

February 28, 4:35 PM

Amy left behind mysteries. I found
this bag crumpled up in a closet,
with just the candle and some dried
pine needles in it.

I have no memory of it... where did
this come from? Why the candle?
Why the pine needles?

She (like so many in her family)
had a marvelous memory, whereas
I have a crappy one, and now she's
not here to remember our life for
me. Queue the tears...

Reflections: This feeling has stuck with me. I've continued to find similar mysteries – things I didn't know we had, things of Amy's I've never seen before and wish I'd been able to ask her about. It's excruciatingly difficult to let go of my desire to know everything about her.

February 28, 8:14 PM

Not surprisingly, while watching the Golden Globes, I lost it watching Taylor Simone Ledward accept a best actor award for her late husband, Chadwick Boseman.

What a thing to have to do.

Reflections: This may be the first time my tears were at least partly about someone else — I can imagine what it was like for Ledward to do that. Layered on top are my feelings about major film awards. I, like many who aspire to a career in film, have imagined what I might say if I had to accept an award at the Golden Globes or the Oscars. As my marriage to Amy went on, this got complicated by my resentment at feeling like she wasn't supporting my writing. You always thank your spouse for their support, and how could I do that if I didn't feel like it was true?[36] I couldn't help thinking of that as Ledward accepted the award.

36 *March 30, 5:25PM*

March 1, 1:28 PM

I'm watching the latest episode of *Stanley Tucci's Searching for Italy*, focusing on the region in northern Italy that's home to Bologna and Modena, and I know Amy would be dying of torture, as he eats his way through fresh ricotta, parmigiana, prosciutto, mortadella, balsamic vinegar, and more.

She loved cheese in particular, often declaring that her ideal dessert was a good cheese plate.

March 2, 12:22 PM

I don't have many photos of Amy, and in what videos I have she's usually offscreen talking to the dogs. She didn't want her face online, and in the past five years she also hated the weight she'd gained from her medical crises, so she probably wasn't keen to have it captured permanently.

And of course, this is heartbreaking for me. I did realize that what I really want from videos is her voice. And to my great relief I discovered I have two short voicemails on my phone from her, AND that I can save them to my computer.

One of those is from her first night in the hospital this last time, and she finishes with "Love you, bye". As you can imagine, being able to hear her voice saying she loves me means every so much.

Reflections: I don't think heartbreaking is a strong enough word to capture how strongly I felt in the moment I thought I didn't have a video of her. It was the worst. I spent the next couple hours desperately looking for recordings, video or audio, with her voice in them. And while it's true that I wanted to hear her voice most of all, with my crappy memory I did also want video of her so I can see her move.[37] My memories tend to be photos rather than video.

37 May 17, 12:23 PM

March 3, 9:27 AM

It was quite a shock to flip the calendar and find an empty month.

Amy was the primary audience for our paper calendars, even after we'd been using shared phone calendars for years. Of course with the pandemic there has been a lot less to calendar, but at the very least Amy would always copy over birthdays when we got the new year's calendar – and for some reason she didn't do that this time.

It's so eerie and sad. The empty page mirrors like what my life feels like without her, but her not copying over birthdays also ties into other changes I'd observed in her over the last year or two, that felt like she was shrinking (or something) in some way. How I wish I knew what she was going through.

Reflections: It's hard not to think of the empty calendar as meaning that on some level she knew she was going to die. It could also be a creepy coincidence. And it's not like she hadn't gotten to it yet – every previous year she'd sat down with the old calendar and new calendar to copy over the birthdays and highlight the flag days. The flag days are highlighted in this calendar, but the birthdays are missing. She didn't say anything to me. So it'll always be a mystery – and a painful one 'til I let go of it.

March 3, 9:07 PM

As Amy died, I forgave her for every angry, sarcastic, judgemental thing she said or did. It just happened inside me as my whole perspective on our relationship dramatically shifted and I realized what really mattered to me.

But despite all the insights I've shared here, forgiving myself is proving much harder.

The truth is that while we had sweet and fun moments, most of the time she seemed either unhappy with me or indifferent, and I'm used to taking that personally – even though I know she was dealing with an unbelievable amount of stuff.

It will probably take some active work for me to fully accept that it wasn't about me, and that she really did feel well-loved.

Reflections: I didn't explicitly, consciously forgive her. It's more like I stopped caring about all the behavior that had upset me before – all I cared about was that we loved each other. I think that abrupt perspective shift came from the fact that I'd have happily put up with the challenges if I could have her back. And that had to mean they weren't important in the first place.

March 4, 6:56 PM

This is Amy's wall at Willamette National Cemetery, where her urn will be interred.[38] I had to walk halfway along it to find someone younger than her.

It's such a stark representation of how many more years we thought we had together. I've cried a lot over that.

I've been trying to focus instead on the time we had, which works out to about 3,030 days. When I think of it that way, it sounds like a lot.

---

38   April 24, 3:22 PM

Reflections: I have clung to that number, 3030 days, ever since — for the same reason. It sounds like a lot. And I need that because it happens so often that I hear a reference to other people having been married for 15, 30, 50 years, and every time it's a stab in my heart.

March 5, 5:44 PM

As I said below,[39] Amy lived and slept in a recliner in our den for most of the past five years. She had too much abdominal discomfort to lie on a bed. Since the den was also the TV room, she had the TV on almost all the time, often even while she slept.

When I got back from the hospital after she died, the TV was off, of course, since no one had been home. And since she wasn't there any more, I left it off except when I was watching. But after a few days I realized that (in addition to her loss, naturally) what felt so off about the house was that it was too quiet. So until today I kept it on during the day.

But today I think she nudged me, and I realized that I might be ready. Today I've had the TV off unless I was watching, and so far it's felt okay. That's a good sign of healing!

This is one of many examples of the difference perspective makes, because it was a pet peeve of mine that she'd leave the TV on while, for instance, she was in the kitchen for an hour. I 'd never have guessed I'd ever need it on.

---

39 February 13, 9:35 PM. On Facebook, I shared my previous post so if anyone needed to read it again to understand the new post, it was right there for them.

March 6, 12:33 PM

And there it is. I get to pay almost $5000 for Amy's death. What an insult that feels like! I am distraught. For all the VA's faults, it and the Oregon Health Plan paid for basically all of Amy's medical expenses when she was using them, hundreds of thousands of dollars – this is the coverage I get through work.

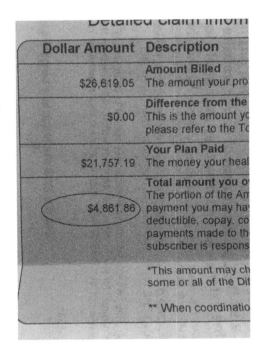

Detailed Claim Inform

Dollar Amount	Description
	Amount Billed
$26,619.05	The amount your pro
	Difference from the
$0.00	This is the amount yc please refer to the To
	Your Plan Paid
$21,757.19	The money your heal
	Total amount you o
$4,861.86	The portion of the An payment you may ha deductible, copay, co payments made to th subscriber is respons
	*This amount may ch some or all of the Dif
	** When coordinatio

Reflections: A bill like this would, of course, be upsetting at any time. The fact that I had a minor meltdown over it was entirely a matter of the grief. Here I was, barely able to work, just getting by, Amy's death still a raw nerve every nanosecond of the day, and I was being asked to pay that much money for the privilege – that's how it felt in the moment. As the days went on, I calmed down, and started playing the insurance game I'd played so often on Amy's behalf. One last time.

March 6, 2:22 PM

Amy just told me to stop apologizing – which is funny because for the first year, I was the one telling her she didn't need to apologize for everything.

And it's true, I regret all the things I've forgotten, or didn't think about, or didn't pay attention to, or...

So, fine, I will stop.

Reflections: It wasn't quite that easy. I still found myself apologizing here and there for months afterward, over things I felt particularly bad about. I'm so used to being keenly aware of how my behavior falls short of my own aspirations, in addition to Amy's unhappinesses. It's been hard to let go of that.

March 6, 4:31 PM

I guess I'll hop on the post-*WandaVision*[40] train, but without (I hope) meaningful spoilers.

Not surprisingly, I sobbed my way through much of the last two episodes. Two moments in particular felt spot on: "I can't feel you" and "To grow old in". The latter hit me because when we bought this house that was how we thought of it. Amy being Amy, a couple years later she decided she wanted to retire to Gearhart instead. And then this fall for some reason she wanted to move to Oregon City. But I never stopped wanting to grow old together in this house, and now I don't get to.

WandaVision exemplifies what I love most about the MCU, and why I find it superior: it embraces the consequences of the actions in its stories. In fact, it's possible that consequences are what fundamentally tie the MCU together. Despite weaknesses in some stories and the over-the-top nature of others, this element gives it all a verisimilitude that really works for me.

---

40 February 18, 9:48 PM

Reflections: The line "I can't feel you" hit me two ways. First, in a literal sense: I can no longer make physical contact with Amy, and this for someone who prizes affection over probably any other expression of love (see next post). Second, in a metaphysical or supernatural sense: some people, including people I know, have the experience of being able to feel a departed loved one's presence, but I haven't experienced that.

March 7, 9:51 PM

Something different happened this morning.

Amy hung her sweatshirts and other over-shirty things on the door to the den, which as I've mentioned is where she basically lived these past five years. Below is the one she was wearing when she went off to the hospital for the last time.

I'm rather touch-oriented (if you're a 'love languages' person, touch is my #1).[41] This shirt has become a kind of tactile surrogate for her, because for several weeks before she died, my experience of touching her usually involved touching this shirt. So every morning, after I let the dogs out, I've been going to this shirt and hugging it – letting the feel of it bring up how desperately I miss Amy, letting waves of longing wash over me, in order to grieve.

This morning, however, after an impromptu in-bed phone call that delayed me starting my day, as I walked toward the den, I felt a message that maybe I didn't need to do my shirt ritual. And the phone call (thanks Honor!) had left me feeling upbeat. So I thought, "okay, we can try that."

I don't see myself making that choice every morning, for now at least.[42] But today it was good to stick with the upbeat way I felt.

---

41 May 1, 9:57 AM

42 April 28, 11:12 AM

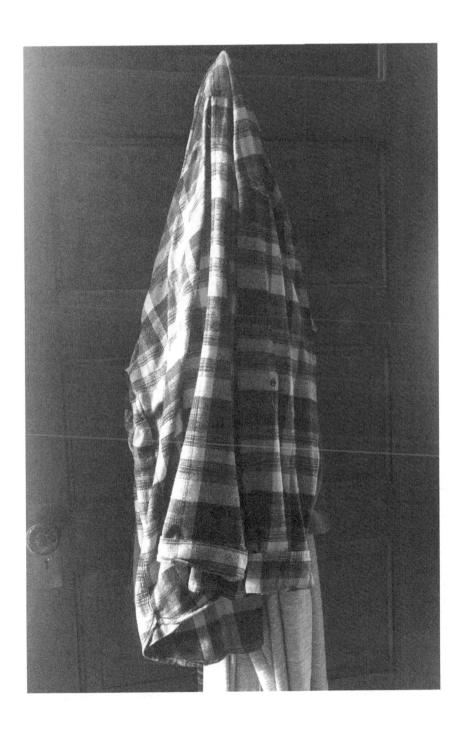

March 8, 9:56 AM

I finally got an obit for Amy into our local paper. This photo was for her 2014 Austin Film Festival badge, and yes, that's a bit of purple in her hair.

Edit: I have to credit Sara for writing a lot of this. She kindly wrote me a draft when I didn't have attention to do so.

columbiagorgenews.com
Obituary: Amy Heil[43]

---

43 The full text of the obituary can be found in the appendix.

Reflections: Once again, I don't know how people do it. I see obits in the paper for people who died that week, yet here I was going on two months later, barely getting one out even with help from someone.

March 9, 8:44 AM

Myra[44] spent a lot of time in Amy's recliner, to the point that it was fairly common for her to jump up there whenever Amy left it.

And somehow, even though it was predictable, each time Amy came back, she would spot Myra there and exclaim "Myra!" as though it were a surprise.

So now it's a comforting thing to see Myra there, as Amy's established recliner surrogate.

---

44 January 27, 6:56 PM

March 9, 6:50 PM

This is Amy's side of the bed. Over the years it got harder for her to sleep in our flat bed[45] (we'd just started talking about replacing it), and even with all these pillows she still had trouble elevating her knees.

So the fact is that it's been at least a year, possible as many as two, since we shared this bed. That was, as you can imagine, hard for both of us; I shed many a tear over it. And it represents yet another perspective flip – what was a source of pain before now makes nights a lot easier.

I truly can't imagine what it's like for someone who's used to sharing a bed to lose that person, and suddenly face an empty bed each night. I'd probably have slept in B's room or the couch.

---

45   February 14, 10:01 PM

Reflections: This is a dramatic understatement of what "Amy's side of the bed" meant for me. Even in the beginning and during her best years, she was rarely able to stay in bed all night twice in a row. She had developed insomnia by 1998 and never shook it, on top of the chronic abdominal pain, nausea, and heartburn she struggled with for decades. Her frequent absence from bed was painful for me – I hated it for the first several years – but by the time I refer to in this post, I had … resigned myself to it, I guess. I never gave up hope, though, nor did she. It meant a great deal to me that in late 2020 she brought up getting a bed with the ability to elevate her head and knees; she hadn't given up either. Ironically, her history with sleeping in our bed made this aspect of her loss much easier for me to deal with.

March 11, 1:35 PM

[The *Food Network*'s "Pioneer Woman"] is one of the cooking shows Amy watched. I find Drummond[46] annoying, but her pandemic episodes can be entertaining since she makes mistakes and gets flustered.

I'm watching an episode in which she makes white chocolate pancakes and smothers them in syrup and whipped cream.

Amy despised white chocolate AND was not a fan of sweetness, so I'm imagining her being grossed out watching it. One more recorded episode to watch, and then I'll say goodbye to the show.

---

46 Ree Drummond, the host of the show; she comes across as delightfully genuine, uttering whatever comes into her head, it seems. In my early childhood, I learned that to survive I had to choose my words carefully, a habit that has remained ingrained in me, so I find it uncomfortable to watch someone doing the opposite.

Reflections: The DVR, second to the kitchen, was probably the most Amy-centric place. She had the TV on all the time, and recorded pretty much every cooking show on the Food Network, along with plenty of other shows. And more than ever, I needed the distraction of watching something while I ate my meals, but having so many episodes of so many shows piling up all the time was enough of a hassle both emotionally and practically, that I probably deleted the recording timers for a lot of shows prematurely — before I was ready to grieve letting them go.

March 11, 3:54PM

In her first winter of college, Amy started this journal, "Things That Mean Something to Me", which initially she populated with quotes from books she read. Over time, she filled it more and more with her own writing.

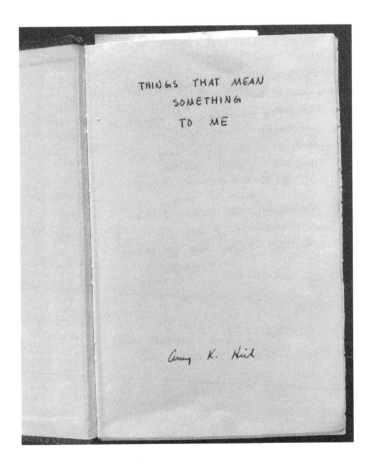

As I thought about how to honor her at her funeral, reading from this book seemed an obvious route. One of my choices was this poem [next page] she included early on. That it would be meaningful to her as a lifelong Christian is no surprise.

Death, Be Not Proud
by John Donne

Death, be not proud, though some have called thee
Mighty and dreadful, for thou art not so;
For those whom thou think'st thou dost overthrow
Die not, poor Death, nor yet canst thou kill me.
From rest and sleep, which but thy pictures be,
Much pleasure; then from thee much more must flow,
And soonest our best men with thee do go,
Rest of their bones, and soul's delivery.
Thou art slave to fate, chance, kings, and desperate men,
And dost with poison, war, and sickness dwell,
And poppy or charms can make us sleep as well
And better than thy stroke; why swell'st thou then?
One short sleep past, we wake eternally
And death shall be no more; Death, thou shalt die.

March 12, 11:38 AM

With the re-addition of work to my life, even part-time, my days are full enough that I often have to remind myself to stop and grieve. There are still plenty of spontaneous upwellings, but it's getting easier to lose track of what I'm going through. I'm sure there's good in that. I just don't want the grieving process to slow down simply because I'm not paying attention.

Right now a lot of the grief focuses on two things: the loss of Amy in the world, and the loss of our future.

When I think of elements like her peace activism, her active support for B, her playfulness, and the way she lit up so many people's lives even through casual social encounters, it feels just so wrong that she's no longer in the world.

And I've mentioned before the need to grieve the future we expected or hoped to have together. To watch B make her way in life and support her in that. To make more short films. To expand the kitchen and our bedroom. To retire to Gearhart on the coast, a place that's been meaningful to Amy since childhood. To keep figuring out how to navigate the tricky waters where our traumas clash. All the movies and concerts and musicals we'd have shared. And so much more. It's overwhelming!

Reflections: *I remember how keenly I felt when I posted this. Deciding to do this book helped with the first of those two things, since through it I feel like Amy's still making the world a better place. The second one ... maybe I've actually let go of it, or maybe I've just gotten better at focusing on deeper levels of grief.*

March 12, 9:20 PM

From the Since the Pandemic Officially Started a Year Ago Department...

Last April, Amy had a cough and a fever, and lost her senses of smell and taste. Her Covid test a couple weeks later came back negative, as did an antigen test in May. Then she had several bouts of pneumonia over summer.

I've seen news reports of other people with negative tests who also had classic Covid symptoms, and I believed all along that Amy had it last April. I also believe it's quite possible that contributed to the suddenness of her death, that it was still rattling around inside her doing its unpredictable damage – her immediate cause of death was that she couldn't breathe, after all.

I've seen some staggering estimates of how many "long haul" Covid victims there are, numbering in the millions. And including people who were asymptomatic initially, but developed serious problems later. So every case of it poses a risk that we can't just dismiss.

Reflections: As I mentioned on January 25, 12:30 PM, I'm more interested in the truth than in comforting thoughts for their own sake, but I'd be naïve to think that only two months after Amy's death, I wasn't desperately wanting to understand why it happened so suddenly, when she'd been stable. It's so much harder to accept a death that seems out of the blue. The possibility of her death was something we had lived with throughout our time together, but there was just no reason to think that she'd up and die at that point. Logically, in order to say she hadn't gotten Covid, you'd have to believe that she had some other much rarer virus with the exact same symptoms as classic Covid – that's just far-fetched. And if she'd had Covid, and shown clear signs of it still affecting her six months later, then it's reasonable to think her organs were weaker as a result. And, as I write this all out, it becomes clear that I still want there to be more of a reason for her dying when she did.

March 13, 9:12 PM

This is the last of the Netflix DVDs from Amy's queue that arrived before she died. Of course I put this one off! Amy wasn't terminally ill, but it's still really close to home. So I mostly cried my way through it.

Amy had put a lot of thought into how she did and didn't want to die. She filed advanced directives (or whatever they're called) with hospitals, and didn't want to go through prolonged suffering.

And we felt differently about these things, which showed up in arguments over when to put an animal down. I never said anything about her preferences for herself, but it would've been agonizing for me to honor her preferences – or for her to honor mine.

What made it even harder to watch this documentary is that it depicts the process my mom used several years ago without my knowing – I never got to say goodbye.

Reflections: Despite all my other feelings about the way Amy died, I am profoundly grateful that I didn't have to make a difficult decision with her facing a slow decline. I can't imagine having had to balance what I know she wanted with what I'd have wanted. I still had to make a decision, but it was an easy one: the doctor said "She's dying on us, and all we can to is switch to comfort care – do we have your permission?" Well, yeah.

March 14, 10:24 AM

This is the last photo of us I could find on my phone, from the solar eclipse in 2017.

It was a fun trip overall, south to the total eclipse zone, but marred by the fact that Amy drank so much she passed out. A lot of my otherwise fun memories of us are marred in a similar way. Yet another thing I have to grieve in order to enjoy my memories fully.

Reflections: Looking at mixed memories like this, I actually think it may not be so much a matter of grieving them as of forgiving Amy for drinking so much then. Or put another way, I suspect I need to let go of the resentment I felt at the time. One route toward that is to focus on compassion for her – she was dealing with so much that she wasn't able to enjoy those moments without being drunk.

March 14, 11:50 AM

It is a curious inversion of the usual reality... normally in order to be ambushed, someone or something must be lurking near us.

But when we're grieving, it is absence that lies waiting to pounce, a void that takes us by surprise.

In this case, I finished reading a *The New Yorker* – which I'm used to now[47] – and on the very last page is an ad for Japanese knives. For years I've had a Japanese knife on my list of gifts to get Amy.

---

47 February 16, 9:42 PM

March 14, 3:47 PM

Today was a painful day to start. Amy almost always marked Pi Day,[48] most memorably with these puppy pies – note the bone shape in the top crust. That was such an Amy thing to do.

---

48 A geeky celebration, on 3/14, of the mathematical number, typically represented as 3.14.

Reflections: I've continued to struggle with special dog-related days, like birthdays. Amy almost always did something special to mark those days, and I just don't know what to do. I feel guilty for doing nothing, but it's probably harder to think about it because all that really comes to mind is how much I miss Amy.

March 14, 9:18 PM

I'd never watched the Grammys until Amy came along. They're my annual reminder of how out of touch I usually am with pop culture.

Amy, of course, was typically up on it all because she was a news and culture junkie. A couple years ago that inspired me to check out the albums on the main iTunes page every so often.

And so it happened last spring that I came across Dua Lipa's album *Future Nostalgia*, and I liked it enough to buy it – though I'd never heard of her before.

Fast forward to last November when this year's Grammy nominations came out – and this album was nominated in five categories. Only then did I discover that Amy liked it too.

But we never got to listen to it together because we only did that on road trips, and I'm not sure Amy even got in the car after that.

So for *Future Nostalgia* to win Best Pop Vocal Album, while I'm watching the Grammys without the woman who led me to hear it in the first place, was rather poignant. Cue tears.

Reflections: There's another layer to this, which is how we related to each other around music. We only ever listened to music together on car trips. And on car trips Amy assumed control of the music by default – she hardly ever asked anyone else what they wanted to listen to. She'd just pick something. When I occasionally pre-empted her, she seemed unhappy about it (though without saying anything direct), and when I or B played something we'd discovered a shared enjoyment of, Amy seemed to resent it. Sometimes I shared a new album I'd found with her, hoping she'd like it, and she never did. That's why the fact that we apparently came to like this album separately gave me hope that I could, for once, get to enjoy with her music I'd found on my own.

March 15, 11:17 AM

Amy's relationship to personal interaction was a complex one. Those of you who contributed memories of her (two months ago now!) used words like "sweet", "warm", "a light", and of course, "funny". And there were times when she wanted to go out just to talk to strangers. Yet she almost always needed alcohol to socialize, and in private she was usually quite different.

I have no doubt that those qualities were genuine.[49] But somewhere along the way, they seem to have gotten wrapped up in trauma, such that they didn't necessarily feel genuine to her, or maybe that it just took more work to get there – which could've made them feel artificial.

She wrote this in 1993, while stationed at Keesler AFB in Biloxi, MS, and excelling in her medical training.

HYPERBOLE

I have no idea where this life of mine is going.
I know too much, and think too much;
I please too much, and always smile.
And if you like me it's because I put on such an act.
I want to be an average Jane,
But every message in and out forces me to shine.
And when the doubt comes with an answering, vengeful swing,
My superficial brilliance is easily consumed.
And so it goes, the tide with time.
A bizarre oscillation of a wave that has no end.
Yet its forces bind me to the path of ebb and flow.
I bounce along it as a flowing live hyperbole.

49 June 4, 11:05 AM

Reflections: The idea that *"if you like me it's because I put on such an act"* is a recurring theme in Amy's writing,[50] at least through 1999. And it certainly relates to what I saw in her during our marriage.

On the one hand, she'd sometimes feel a need to get out and socialize — which usually meant sitting at a bar, drinking, and talking to the person next to her — while on the other hand, she rarely followed up on the connections she made that way. Making connections, or what seemed like connections, with people seemed easy for her, yet she had few friends. She could pick up the phone in the middle of a screaming argument with me, and be perfectly composed and pleasant to the caller. At the time, all together, it did leave me wondering sometimes which was the real Amy.

50 February 12, 10:56 AM

March 15, 2:19 PM

A whole new source of grief just walloped me like a rogue wave.

In 2013, right at the beginning of our marriage, Amy and I suffered a miscarriage.[51] He would've been Wolf Owen Worsley, a WOW to B's BOW[52] – her idea.

And now his mama is gone too. It's almost too much.

---

51 June 20, 10:41 AM

52 Brooklyn's initials

Reflections: This one is still almost too much. In the ocean of my grief, there is an entire sea devoted to "Now there's no one who really knows what I went through." Not that I'm alone in suffering these losses, but rather, every situation is unique. Amy and I shared the burden of losing Wolf, and we frequently reminded each other of how often we felt his loss. Now the burden is entirely mine. This is big enough that I might need to take special steps to deal with it – find a miscarriage support group, or start one.

March 16, 4:15 PM

This prayer of mourning from Jewish liturgy[53] (thanks, Simone!) is
beautiful, and I'm sure Amy would've agreed wholeheartedly. It also
captures what I aspire to do for her.

> When I die give what's left of me away
> to children and old men that wait to die.
> And if you need to cry,
> cry for your brother walking the street beside you.
> And when you need me, put your arms around anyone
> and give them what you need to give me.
>
> I want to leave you something,
> something better than words or sounds.
> Look for me in the people I've known or loved,
> and if you cannot give me away,
> at least let me live in your eyes and not in your mind.
>
> You can love me best by letting hands touch hands,
> and by letting go of children that need to be free.
> Love doesn't die, people do.
> So, when all that's left of me is love,
> give me away.

---

53 *Mishkan T'Filah: A Reform Siddur*. New York, Central Conference of American
Rabbis, 2007, p. 288.

Reflections: This has lost none of its power for me. And now that I think of it, "giving Amy away" is a complement to "letting go of Amy." I can't cling to her and give her away at the same time. Given who she was and what she valued, how can I justify keeping her to myself when giving her away will make the world a better place? Of course, it's easy to give away her things, and to share who she was and what she wrote ... what exactly it would mean to give her away, that will take some work and time to figure out.

March 16, 7:04 PM

Even after two months, the finality of Amy's death is still sinking in. After I sat with her during her last hour. After I watched the nurse confirm that her heart had stopped. After her funeral – and so on. How can it really be?

Now we have this, Amy's obituary.[54] I wrote it with Sara's help,[55] but seeing it in the paper... holy crap that hits me. I got the paper two days ago, and I couldn't look at it until today.

OBITUARIES

PAID NOTICES

Amy Heil

Amy Heil

Amy Katherine Heil (formerly Williams) was born in Portland, Ore., in 1970, the fifth and youngest child of F. Charles W. Heil and Patricia Willard Heil. She passed away unexpectedly on Jan. 13, 2021, with her husband, John Worsley, at her side.

Known in the family as "Amy Kat," Amy was raised in southwest Portland. She attended West Hills Christian and soon-to-be-formerly-known-as Wilson High School, where she sang in the choir and wrote for the school newspaper. She was a bright and creative student who, if all her stories are to be believed, must've had 40-hour days. She studied Political Science at Bard College in New York and at Reed College before joining the US Air Force in 1991. While on active duty, she also completed her bachelor's degree at William Carey College.

Amy's eight-year career as a medical technician took her to Texas, Mississippi, Japan, and California. She took every opportunity to excel and exceeded every limit placed before her. Upon leaving the Air Force, she returned to Portland, where she married Justin Williams. Their daughter, Brooklyn, is Amy's pride and joy. In 2005, the family moved to the Hood River area where Amy and Justin opened a successful restaurant, Sushi Okalani; the restaurant's logo is an example of Amy's artistic work.

In 2013, she married John Worsley, and the new family moved to Mosier later that year so Brooklyn could attend Mosier Community School. Amy supported the charter school enthusiastically, filling their home with art purchased at benefit auctions. She was also the creative force behind two short films she made with John, "Mayhem in Mosier" (2014) and "All Our Sins Remembered" (2016). The latter film won Best Adaptation at the 2016 Columbia Gorge International Film Festival.

As a Quaker, Amy worked passionately for peace, volunteering virtually for the Friends Committee on National Legislation as well as Veterans for Peace, and attending rallies, protests, and marches. She wrote a number of opinion pieces for the Hood River News promoting peace and understanding.

Amy had a playful sense of humor, loved to tell stories, almost invariably charmed those who met her, loved to foster rescue dogs, and was proud of being a "softie" who cried at car commercials.

She will be remembered forever by her husband, John Worsley, of Mosier; her daughter, Brooklyn Williams; her daughter-in-spirit, Alison Dye; and by Justin Williams. She is also survived by her father, Chuck; her four siblings and their spouses; her nieces and nephew; and her beloved aunt, Margaret Heil. Amy was a devoted pet mom to three Welsh corgis, Myra, Meatloaf, and Merlin.

A private funeral service was held for family on February 26 at Willamette National Cemetery.

---

54   The full text of the obituary can be found in the appendix.

55   March 8, 9:56 AM

March 17, 10:38 PM

Thoughts for today...

For Amy's virtual memorial, I've desperately wanted to fully represent each part of her life, especially having someone present who was part of it. Until today I was missing that for her years in Japan, which she loved and which stayed with her the rest of her life. After hours of web searching, trying to find the one friend I knew of from then, I ended up writing a snail mail letter to an address I had to pay a personal info site to get – and tonight I got to talk to him. It means SO much to have someone to fill in some of the pieces of her development as a person.

My mourning process seems more and more to include tears of gratitude to Amy for how much she gave me in so many ways, from our beautiful home to my love for the Columbia River Gorge to her sense of humor to her gentle devotion to peace, and so on, culminating, of course, with my connection to B.

Reflections: Tears of gratitude for all that Amy gave me have become a regular part of my end-of-day ritual. This marks a dramatic shift from my experience of life with her. I did try to find gratitude for Amy at least once a day,[56] but much of the time I was full of unhappiness and resentment over what I wanted but felt I couldn't have because of her. I'm still working on letting go of wishing I'd been able to see back then how much she was giving me.

56 January 24, 11:54 AM

March 18, 12:07 PM

I have to give special credit to this show for getting me through the first month of grieving. I had no interest in doing much of anything, and almost everything I could think to watch (and would *want* to watch) was either something Amy and I shared, or something I had to watch by myself because she wasn't interested.

Monty Python's Flying Circus occupied a rare niche, in being something that had no Amy factor to it. She was a fan in the general sense that many people are, but we never watched it together, and I had only discovered it's on Netflix just before her death. So it was magically Amy-neutral, and

© Python (Monty) Pictures Limited.

almost the only thing I could stand to watch for the first couple weeks.

Since I was incapable of enjoying anything, it was weird to watch and not find anything funny – but that actually cleared the way for a deeper appreciation for their creativity than I'd had before.

March 19, 5:51 PM

This is Amy's phone. In the last two
months there hasn't been anything in any
of her apps or her email – or even a phone
call – that has been personal or needed a
response.

I find that depressing. I keep hoping some
interaction will pop up, some sign that
there are more people out there who want
to interact with her.

It feeds into my sense that her life these
last couple years had contracted – which
in turn makes me wonder what she was
dealing with that she never told me. She
rarely went into much detail about her
physical or emotional struggles, with me
anyway. And now I'll never know.

Reflections: Someone pointed out that perhaps I wasn't seeing any communications because I'd done a great job of contacting people in her life. It's a fair point. It does not, however, cover the pain I felt from how isolated Amy often seemed to me, as I commented on for March 15, 11:17 AM.

March 20, 9:40 PM

I've posted before about feeling emotionally homeless.[57] It's a messy affair... when I left Portland to join Amy in the Gorge, she was planning (or at least seriously talking about) moving back to Portland to study at George Fox University.

I'd lived in Portland for 23 years at that point, and it was home, so leaving it was a big deal. Having the sense that we'd be back in Portland in the foreseeable future played a big part in my decision to move.

But one thing I now know about her is that, given time to keep pondering plans, she'd often change her mind. So by the time a couple years had passed, she wanted to stay here. And that was hard for me. I'd given up almost my entire life to be with her.

And now over eight years later, Portland has changed a lot. It certainly doesn't feel like home, though I have many friends there. But without Amy, this place doesn't feel like home either – I certainly don't have enough friends here.

It's not a conundrum I feel the need – or the ability – to figure out now, but it does get in the way of being able to envision myself being happy.

When it's safe for you to do so, you are ALL invited to visit!

---

57 February 18, 11:10 AM

Reflections: My aunt gave me the advice early on not to make any big decisions until at least a year has passed, and that made sense to me. But it was hard not to question my place in the world, and people tended to ask me if I was going to stay here. The only reason I ended up here was Amy, so it was a fair question. Happily, as time has passed I've regained my feeling of this being my home – which underscores the advice about not making big decisions too soon.

March 21, 10:40 PM

Amy gave me this guardian angel pendant a few weeks after we got together. I was still living in Portland and spending three days a week with her, so it represented her wish for me to have a safe drive.

She would 'charge it up' with a kiss every so often. After I moved out here, I wore it the one day a week I drove out to Tigard for work. Once that job ended and I rarely went anywhere without her, she gradually lost her attachment to it. But I, being me, never did. I continued to wear it whenever I drove into Portland without her, and would still give it to her to kiss sometimes – getting in return a 'you sweet, sentimental man' look.

Needless to say, I'll keep wearing it for drives, just with a different meaning – like taking Amy with me.

Reflections: What I mean by "I, being me, never did" is an important question. I don't feel I've found quite the right words to capture this prominent character trait. I could say it's about commitment, that when I commit to something I take the commitment absolutely seriously. I could say I was devoted to Amy – that's certainly a common way to express it. Maybe Amy put it best with "sweet, sentimental." I do know that once she had invested something with meaning, I never let go of that meaning, even if she did. She once told me early on that if I opened her car door for her – a stereotypical "chivalrous" act I resisted initially – she'd always thank me for it. I kept doing it long after she took it for granted.

March 22, 7:26 PM

In a similar vein to my post about emotional homelessness,[58] I also feel like I don't exactly know who I am now.

I've always been an adaptable person who can enjoy things because other people do. I hadn't watched any sports for 30+ years when Amy and I got together, but it was easy to share her love of football. Now I have no idea what I'll do with the next football season.

That's just one specific example. More broadly, Amy wasn't able to do paid work while we were married. There were times when she applied for jobs, but her unstable health would've made it hard to keep a job. And it's been five years since I had an office job.

So we've both been home together for five years, with little separation in what we did (in part because Amy really disliked it when I did things without her, unless it was due to her health). The result is that who I am has been defined almost exclusively in the context of Amy.

It'll be a long road, sorting through what I truly want to keep of who I've been with Amy, vs. what it would feel unfaithful to stop being (hello, extreme loyalty), vs. who I want to be.

58　March 20, 9:40 PM

....

Reflections: "vs. what it would feel unfaithful to stop being": I'm referring to the same character trait as in the previous post. My feeling here seems to be that I need to stay the same person I was with Amy or I'm somehow letting her down, or betraying her, or something like that. It sounds so illogical when I put into words like that, but – welcome to feelings. This one, though, seems to have lessened over time. I've reinvented myself before – in college, for instance, when I realized that no one there had any preconceived notions about who I was – so I can do it again. And knowing Amy wants me to be happy counteracts the pull to somehow "stay the same" for her. On a more fundamental level, the healing I'm experiencing through my grieving process is bound to lead to change.

March 23, 7:52 PM

These are voicemail messages on Amy's phone. I've been putting off listening to them, until tonight.

Amy's beloved Auntie M called the day Amy went to the hospital – she didn't know Amy was there, and was just calling to check in as she did every so often. It's heartbreaking that Amy was too gorked out to listen to it.

And Lisa is Amy's sister, who left that tearful message after I alerted the family to the fact that Amy was in danger – but before we knew just how much in danger she was. At least Lisa got to be on the phone with me for Amy's final moments.

Greeting		Edit
Voicemail		
● **Lisa D** mobile	1/12/21 00:36	ⓘ
● **Auntie M** mobile	1/10/21 00:42	ⓘ
+1 (503) 494-4... Portland, OR	12/28/20 00:25	ⓘ
Unknown unknown	12/17/20 02:23	ⓘ
Unknown unknown	12/14/20 00:29	ⓘ

But they're both agonizing reminders of all the goodbyes that didn't get said.

Reflections: I think "goodbyes that didn't get said" fall into the realm of taking people for granted. "Oh well, I didn't get to see you today, but next year I will." It's such a human thing to do. What would it really look like if we didn't assume we'll have the future to appreciate the people in our lives? Would that be sustainable? Would it become overwhelming if we all did it? These are questions I imagine I'll be pondering for some time to come.

March 24, 8:03AM

As I watch TV, I try to enjoy it the way I would with Amy, making observations and jokes – and sometimes I do bust out laughing, knowing Amy would be laughing too.

But that laughter is always followed by a burst of tears, because she's not actually here. I don't get to look over and see the look on her face, or laugh at her surprising wisecrack.

Still, I'll keep trying, because otherwise all I have is the pain.

Reflections: And I have kept trying, and it's gotten easier. The laughter still comes, and now it's followed by a pang of sadness, but not enough to dull my enjoyment. The full picture is that within the first few days after Amy's death, I started talking out loud to myself in certain circumstances – something I used to do. In part, for both these cases, my motivation was that I wanted avoid getting used to keeping my thoughts to myself, because at some point in the future I'd presumably have someone around to share my thoughts with.

March 25, 3:35 PM

As I expected, Myra has been the only one noticeably affected by Amy's disappearance (as it must seem to her).

After a couple weeks, she stopped coming downstairs in the morning to go outside. She just goes belly-up, ears back, full submission "please don't make me". So I let her come down when she's ready – which is for breakfast, and then she goes out.

And she's coming upstairs a lot more to hang out with me, since there's often no one downstairs.

I wish I could tell her that Mama's never coming back, so she doesn't keep hoping in whatever doggy way she does.

Then again, part of me still has trouble with that...

Reflections: "trouble with that" meaning, not literally that I was hoping Amy would come back, but how hard it has been to accept that she's really gone. It happened so suddenly, I had no time to come to grips with knowing I was going to lose her, and only one night to get used to even the possibility of it. I still sometimes feel a wave of "How can you be gone, just like that?" wash over me.

March 27, 9:47 AM

Amy often added items to the shopping list that she intended to use at some point, even without a specific meal plan for them.

Thus I now have these two unopened but expired cheese packages; the queso fresco's date is from September. Cheese is one of my food sensitivities, so even if they're still usable, it just doesn't make sense for me.

Amy hated wasting food, as do I. And of course the idea of tossing these Amy relics carries an extra burden... but I don't see a viable alternative.

Reflections: This is really about wanting to cling to Amy, and about feeling like I was letting her down by wasting food.

March 28, 7:54 AM

I'm just starting to realize that in addition to all the pain and sorrow, I have some terror to process – coming from the moment I heard the doctor say Amy was dying. That is the closest I've come to having a panic attack.

I was in the bathroom at the time, and I sank down onto the floor. No idea how long I stayed there. It'll probably take some choice on my part to face that moment fully, since it's easier to feel pain than terror.

Reflections: I've occasionally let myself go there since this post, but it's so much easier just to forget that moment is still there, waiting for my attention.

March 28, 3:58 PM

I opened the glove box in the car to replace the insurance card, and found an emotional minefield. Since I did all the driving, that was Amy's side of the car. The numbered items require explanation.

1. Amy had been so sick when we got together that she had an official disabled placard. Overall, we used it less as time went on, but she really did need it a fair amount. I suspect, however, that she was happy to let it lapse, because she desperately wanted to feel more normal.

2. The spray top to a Narcan bottle she was prescribed in Sept., after her first alcoholic hepatitis. That was the first time she'd been prescribed Narcan to go with her opioids, and I'm glad on principle that it was included – although Amy didn't need it. Despite confessing to an addictive personality and her longtime alcohol dependence, prescription medication was never a problem for her, and she usually got off opioids faster than planned.

3. Two receipts from Goodwill that she stashed in there, where they were forgotten.

4. This is a puzzle to me. Why was she keeping a slightly smoked cigar in the car? The only time she ever smoked her cigars or cigarillos was a couple times a year when she was angry at me, and that was always on the patio.

5. On the left, barf bags, and on the right, a collection of anti-nausea and anti-heartburn meds along with OTC[59] painkillers. All that was in addition to the stash she always carried in her purse. She didn't need all of it all the time, but between pain, nausea, and vomiting, there wasn't a lot of time she was reliably safe from all three.

---

59 Over the counter

March 29, 8:09 AM

I woke up to snow on the hills, which reminded me how much Amy loved snow. She would stand at the window looking out, saying "I want snow!"

After the brief round we had on Christmas, I'd been practicing the harmonizing line "Snow, snow, snow, snow, snow!" from *Holiday Inn*, and looking forward to singing that to her next time it snowed.

But by the time the next snow came, she was gone.

Reflections: The movie I was thinking of is actually White Christmas (I tend to confuse the two films), which I was raised with and presumably planted in me the lifelong magic I associate with the idea of a snowy Christmas. I retained my love of snow all through nine years living in the Northeast. So Amy and I shared that love, and now I think of her every time I see snow, which makes it all the more special.

March 30, 7:58 AM

I just discovered that Amy had a Tumblr account. She only posted a handful of times in 2015, all photos of Myra.

And she only followed two people: me, though oddly she didn't Like any of my posts of faces I'd noticed in the world, and a corgi account called CorgiAddict whose posts she did Like.

It sure looks to me like she got on Tumblr to follow CorgiAddict. So many mysteries... I don't like it. It contributes to my feeling that I didn't know her as well as I thought I did.

~little derper, little derper girl...~

Reflections: Friends pointed out that partners don't usually know everything the other is doing online. And sure, Amy would've encountered a lot more of these "surprises" if our situations were reversed. But I don't think the problem is really one of feeling like I didn't know her as well as I thought I did. Amy kept a lot to herself, mostly about what she was feeling, going through, struggling with. She rarely asked for help and rarely took advice that was offered. And that was painful for me, to be right here with her, sharing a life, wanting to know what was going on inside her, and being so often denied. I think discovering that she had online activity she didn't mention feeds into that struggle of mine.

March 30, 5:25PM

This is the hardest day I've had in at least a month, and the first time I've experienced my grief suddenly getting a lot stronger. I'm surprised, actually, at how relatively linear it's been so far.

I've re-evaluated my sense of Amy's support for my writing. It was hard for me to carve out writing time because it always came out of time I'd otherwise have been with her, and she was a needy person who usually wanted me with her.

The truth is, I resented her for that. Screenwriting is my passion and was our only real hope for retirement income, and she rarely encouraged me. Most of the time she tolerated, at best, my desire to go off and write; it felt like if it were up to her, I'd only write occasionally. She also sometimes made snide comments about "whatever you're doing up there." But last fall I did decide to prioritize time with her more, and gave up on some writing time – and I'm glad I did that. I think it made a difference for her as her health was worse than it had been for a while.

What I see now is that her general enthusiasm for watching movies – particularly back when she was up for "movie days" in Portland when we'd see three or four movies – as well as her desire to make short films with me, was in fact enormously supportive of me. It's yet another area that meant much more to me than I realized until now. I'm determined to learn something about perspective from all this.

Reflections: The fact is, while I watched more movies than most people before Amy and I got together, and while I'd had exposure – thanks to my mom and to one particular friend in my youth – to a wider array of movies than most people, I didn't consider myself a movie buff in any sense, and I mostly watched genre movies and period pieces back then. Amy turned me into a movie buff, into someone who keeps a list of movies he reads about and wants to see and who watches a lot of independent films, who can form opinions about Oscar nominees because he's seen most of them. And that is invaluable, something I'll always be deeply grateful to Amy for.

March 30, 8:12 PM

I love [the 2009 movie *Moon*] enough that I bought the blu-ray a while ago. I wanted to share it with Amy, but her fear of asphyxiation kept her from watching many space movies.

Yet she recorded it this past fall, so I knew she wanted to see it. I kept insisting it deserved our living room projector screen rather than our much smaller TV, with the result that we never watched it.

So it's been on the DVR till now. And you bet I regret not letting Amy watch it the way she wanted to. I don't think I was paying enough attention to how much she was struggling.

I finally deleted it just now, in a burst of sobbing. And again, I'm determined to learn.

Reflections: This was as much about forgiving myself as about letting go. Forgiving myself if only because I knew Amy forgives me. As for being determined to learn, at the time it didn't occur to me to wonder why she didn't want to watch the movie on our projector screen. I think there was enough I already resented her for that I just (unconsciously) added this to the list, and I don't want to repeat that behavior.

March 31, 8:01 AM

I've mentioned that Amy was a news junkie.[60] I don't mean that in a pejorative sense – politics and what goes on in the world were important to her as early as high school.

Whenever possible, she'd go for original sources of information so she could assess the reporting of it. This meant watching every minute of key trials, debates, speeches, etc.

Derek Chauvin's trial in Minneapolis started Monday for the death of George Floyd, so CNN has been showing a lot of live video from it.

My first impulse is to feel like watching that live trial video isn't an efficient use of my time. But I'm letting Amy challenge me to do what she did – see for myself what happens rather than letting someone else characterize it for me. So I'm watching it.

_____

60   March 14, 9:18 PM

Reflections: This is a confusing thing to balance. On the one hand, I think there's value in honoring the way Amy pushed me to be more aware of what's going on in the world. On the other hand, there's an unhealthy way to do it: use "doing what she did" as a way of avoiding letting go. I don't know that there's a magic bullet to solve the problem, though I do know one sign of the unhealthy approach – rigidity. I don't have to do any one thing to honor Amy, nor do I need to feel guilty if I don't do something she'd've done. I'll have to pay close attention when I make these choices.

March 31, 2:46 PM

Amy and I married eight years ago today. It was a simple affair in the Crystal Springs Rhododendron Garden in southeast Portland, with just us, Brooklyn, and my parents (Simone signed the paperwork). And it was a beautiful spring day, with flower petals raining down on us from the blossoming trees.

We kept it simple because for each of Amy's previous two weddings, the groom's family had pressured her into huge to-dos; I was happy to let her do it the way she wanted.

We'd been together for six months by then, with three more months of reconnecting before that, but we'd made enough connection in college to have written a couple sweet letters, and I visited her in Biloxi on my cross-country trip in 1992.

Still, we did move fast. And by the time of the wedding, Amy's behavior to me had changed a lot. Where she'd been almost universally positive before, she was critical, sarcastic, and easily upset. Now, the miscarriage had already happened, so it could've just been due to that, but she never did get back to where she started. There were dark moments over the years in which I thought we'd've been better off waiting, getting to know each other more deeply.

It also occurred to me in more upbeat times that Amy was unconsciously expecting me to leave her, turn on her, or something like that, and was trying to get that over with as soon as possible. I do think that was part of it, in tandem with stuff I've posted about before.[61]

We were planning to be at Timberline Lodge tonight, but since the Edgefield Hotel was our favorite place, I'm honoring the occasion by meeting friends for an outdoor dinner there. Happy anniversary, my love.

---

61 February 12, 10:56 AM / February 14, 11:06 AM

Reflections: Oh boy. So much more I could say here, but what stands out the most is that I don't remember much from our wedding, which hurts. The flower petals standing in for rice or whatever else people might throw — that I remember, because it was magical. Pretty high on my list of what I'd have asked Amy, if we'd had any time before she died, is "What did we say for vows?" One of countless things I didn't need to remember as long as I had Amy, because she had a fantastic memory for events and places.

April 1, 5:53 PM

We have two refrigerators and a freezer, and they were often all full with Amy around. She cooked more often than I have been, but she also just kept more on hand.

All three of them are emptying out. At this point I'm much more of a "buy it when I need it" person, and I've also been partly choosing meals to make based on what we have, just because it's easier and I need easier.

But the gradual emptying makes me sad. I want Amy to be here, doing the thing she loved so much. I want to be able to come up behind her in the kitchen, put my head on her shoulder, and watch what she's doing for a few seconds – till she shrugs me off because "I'm working here". Cooking always took priority over affection.[62]

---

62 May 1, 9:57 AM

Reflections: Coming up behind and resting our head on the other's shoulder was something we did to each other in various situations. When I say "affection" here, I mean "physical affection" – a conflation that says a lot about how oriented I am to physical affection.

April 2, 5:34 PM

I had another unexpected Amy-voice-in-my-head experience.[63] I was showering, and crying as I always do now – because it's one of the few reliable points in the day when I can stop and feel.

I was focusing on the thought that we had a good life together, and suddenly a voice in my head said, "promise you'll have a good life in the future too!"

At the moment, still deep in the grief, that's a tall order. But I managed to muster this: I promise to reach for promising that I'll have a good life in the future too.

---

63 February 24, 6:15 PM

Reflections: I don't remember this moment. That might speak to how hard it was for me to have ramped back up to close-to-full time at work around this point; I was doing it, but not doing it well, and it was taking a lot out of me. But now I can promise that I'll have a good life in the future too.

April 3, 9:46 PM

Another re-evaluation... the combination of me leaving my home of 20+ years (Portland) to join Amy in her life, plus her need to feel in control, plus her insecurity, led to me adapting a lot to how she wanted things to be. To a certain extent that came easily to me, and in other ways it left me feeling resentful.

But it suddenly hit me... before we got together, I highly doubt Amy would've identified as a geek in the usual sense (perhaps in high school?). As a literary geek, maybe, or a political geek – some qualified, specific sense – but not in the unqualified cultural sense. Well, she certainly married one in me, and I think my presence encouraged B in her nascent geekhood. And Amy went with it.

I'll never know how much of this she'd have done just for me, versus how much she did just for B. ... I started writing this a couple hours ago, and I've lost some of the thoughts that prompted me to post! I could list specific things she joined me in enjoying, like *Doctor Who*, but the point is a more general one. She did more than just tolerate my geeky enjoyment of things; she got into some of them with me.

Okay, not my most organized or eloquent post, but I want to give Amy credit for making room in our relationship for this key part of who I am.

Reflections: In all fairness, I have a lifelong habit of adapting my behavior, my expression of myself, to the people I'm around. And Amy's sister Lisa says they were a family of geeks who watched Doctor Who growing up, so it may have more to do with Amy's need to feel like she was taken seriously, or something like that. But whether she was hiding an inherent geekiness or lacking it doesn't affect my point, which is that she embraced it with me and for her daughter. As for this not being my most organized or eloquent post, the word I was looking for was actually coherent – coherence in how I communicate is vitally important to me. See the previous day's reflection on work's effect on me.

April 4, 10:07 PM

Amy wrote the poem below in 1993, when she was stationed in Biloxi, MS, and excelling at every opportunity. I think the act she refers to putting on became, at some point, her default way of interacting – as though she didn't know what else to do to meet her need for human connection.

And by the time we reconnected, it seems as though the strain of doing something that felt less than real, in order to meet a real need, required alcohol to manage. And for me, in turn, the role of alcohol in most of my social experiences with Amy leaves me with confusing memories that are a mix of enjoyment and unhappiness.

HYPERBOLE

I have no idea where this life of mine is going.
I know too much, and think too much;
I please too much, and always smile.
And if you like me it's because I put on such an act.
I want to be an average Jane,
But every message in and out forces me to shine.
And when the doubt comes with an answering, vengeful swing,
My superficial brilliance is easily consumed.
And so it goes, the tide with time.
A bizarre oscillation of a wave that has no end.
Yet its forces bind me to the path of ebb and flow.
I bounce along it as a flowing live hyperbole.

Reflections: *I'd utterly forgotten that I'd posted this same poem just three weeks prior. [64] Since my mind usually does an excellent job tracking whether I've posted something before on Facebook, even from years ago, I can only chalk this up to the toll it was taking on me to have to work.*

64 *March 15, 11:17 AM*

April 5, 9:33 PM

I've been continuing an Amy tradition, of not quite latching the door when using the downstairs bathroom, then when Myra almost inevitably pushes in, exclaiming "Myra, I don't need your help!"

Yes, this is a dirty bathtub. It's Amy's dirt. She had a remarkably clean body that didn't require regular washing, and it's been years since she could comfortably take a bath, but she'd sit on a stool to wash sometimes – or maybe exfoliate... I'm actually not sure what she did while sitting on the stool, because she somehow managed to do it without my knowing.

The dead centipede is a nod to the times she'd tell me about some spider that was stuck in the tub, who she'd named and had conversations with.

The sponge is also called a loofah, and "loofah" was a term of endearment she used to call me – stemming from a story involving a Storm Large concert and Amy misreading (I think) the word "lover" on Storm's shirt.[65]

---

65 May 5, 11:44 AM

Reflections: If I were to feel embarrassed about any of my grief posts, it would be this one. I was attached to her body dirt? But it's true – I wanted to cling to every iota of Amy, since nevermore would any new Amy iota come into being. And this residue of her bathing reminded me that she had to sit on a stool to wash herself, which stemmed from her not being well, which made me think of her drinking and her inability to take advice... and so on. This dirt stood for a lot, as most things still did at this point in my grieving.

April 6, 5:50 PM

Since mid-January I've found several things Amy was missing, including her favorite nail clippers (buried in the basket by her chair), her second pair of reading glasses (fallen into the trashcan by her chair) – and this, her favorite hat (and mine).

As you can see by the photo of her and a very young B, she's had it a while. I don't know where she got it, but it disappeared a couple years ago and we were both sad about that.

Turns out that it, too, was buried, under a pile of hats in the coat closet. I found it, and the other two things, because I've just been looking everywhere she had stuff stored, or anywhere she was in charge of.

Part of me would rather this hat still be missing, because what's the point of finding it if Amy isn't here to wear it? I miss her so much the fullness of it still takes my breath away.

Reflections: Once again, I was desperate for every iota of Amy. Every time I found a surprise, it made me want to keep looking. Finding this hat, though, that hurt. The "why?" of it was overwhelming – why couldn't we have found it years ago? I don't know why she stopped wearing her hats; if she'd been wearing the others, she'd have found this one. I've let go of a lot of the Whys since then, and this hat sits on the shrine that is still Amy's desk. [66]

[66] July 10, 9:53 AM

April 7, 8:59 AM

It's not just that "little" things can trigger grief... they can easily tap into much larger issues.

Case in point: I spilled some water on the dining room floor, and cast about for the nearest thing to soak it up with, which happened to be a dinner napkin. So I used that, then realized there was more water, and got another napkin.

Only then did I realize that the first napkin had been folded in half and set on top of the other napkins.

Which is what Amy did. When we ate at the table, she (or sometimes I) would set out a folded paper napkin with the utensils, and if a napkin went unused, she would put it back on the pile, still folded.

Which means that napkin has been sitting there since she was alive, and she may well have touched it. I burst into tears at that, but my feelings quickly attached to this idea: the world as it was when she lived is slowly, piece by piece, disappearing. And that is a deeper level of pain.

But it doesn't even stop there, because that reminded me that I can't bear the idea of Amy being forgotten – ever – and I'm *desperate* to find a way to preserve some memory of her after I'm gone.

April 7, 5:27 PM

Well. 2021 seems determined to continue upending my life... but it's not all bad.

TL;DR[67]: I'm leaving my job. And going after writing.

I was the second employee at this company, and this past year+ has been the perfect arrangement for me, making a good salary at 30 hours a week, doing something I mostly enjoyed, while leaving me extra time to write.

But the company is growing and its needs are changing, so in the face of being required to work 40+ hours for the same pay while having to commute into Portland 2-3 days a week, I chose instead to resign with severance.

At first I was overwhelmed and upset and panicked about this choice. If I'd stayed under those conditions, it would mean, to me, living in order to work. And I can't do that. I want too much else out of my life. So it was clear I had to leave, but job hunting has been so difficult and mostly fruitless, and I was worried about facing that again.

Then it occurred to me, after a good talk with my sister, that what this actually gives me is an opportunity like I've never had before. For the first time, I have the magic combination of time, flexibility, and – at least through the end of the year, thanks to stunning generosity – money. I really couldn't ask for a better setup to launch my screenwriting career.

So I'm taking a leap of faith. I don't know if I'm quite ready to pick up my writing again – I haven't tried yet – but getting to put it first in my life rather than having to fit it in around the edges of my life... that should energize me big time. Writing movie scripts (and possibly now comics too) is my passion, one of the things I feel like I'm here on earth to do. Now I'm going to go for it, for real.[68]

---

67 An internet abbreviation for "Too long; didn't read."

68 April 21, 5:28 PM

Reflections: Missing from this is how utterly confusing it was, and how utterly conflicted I felt, to find myself in this ideal circumstance because my wife died. It's the sort of circumstance I'd wanted for more than a decade, but how could I want it now, given the cost? Of course I'd give this opportunity up if I could have Amy back! But it doesn't work that way. Also weighing on me was Amy's chronic worry about being a burden. For example, where early on she clung to every minute she could have with me during hospitalizations, recently she'd often urge me to get out, take a break, meet a friend — in other words, to not let her health take over my life. So it was easy to feel like seizing this opportunity would prove that worry justified. But worry about her feelings isn't something I have to carry around any more.

April 8, 10:06 AM

I've been checking Amy's email in case something comes in that requires action, or in the off chance someone from her past emails her. I've mentioned her email habits before[69] – she let most email go to her junk folder. Some of it belongs there, for sure, but a lot of it is legitimate stuff she signed up for.

So I've been marking those as safe. I want them in her inbox so it's easier for me to identify what might matter. I'm not in a hurry to pare it all down to the minimum, because the emails that meant something to her – political activism, for instance – are something I'll need to grieve when I unsubscribe. But it doesn't make sense for her to keep getting emails from places she just ordered something from once, so I've been unsubscribing from them.

And yet even though I want to do this, each time I unsubscribe her from, say, emails from Chewy, I hit that last button and it feels like being forced to say, "Yes, my wife is dead." The fact that I feel it so strongly for these insignificant unsubscribes just highlights why I'm not ready to tackle the significant ones. Maybe I never will, who knows. Amy was proud of her vintage Hotmail address from 1999.

---

69   February 22, 2:47 PM

Reflections: I gradually got her inbox whittled down to emails that mean something, and so I find myself reading her email once a day. I've signed myself up for a few newsletters she gets, figuring that if I'm willing to read them via her account, I'll be willing to do so via mine. But it's still true that when I unsubscribe her from something, and get that "tell us why you're leaving" choice, part of me wants to choose Other and type in "I'm dead" – not to be mean, but because it still hurts to have to do this at all, and being forced to confront the Why of it sure makes the pain worse.

April 8, 12:53 PM

A couple dozen reminders that Amy wasn't well. I *think* that's everything. I'm ready to drop them off at a safe disposal site.

As much as I cry about missing her, I also cry about how much she suffered, and about how free she is now, from pain, discomfort, fear, self-loathing, etc.

So I don't really feel attached to these objects – they were hardly an intrinsic part of her. But they will still be tear-stained by the time I part with them.

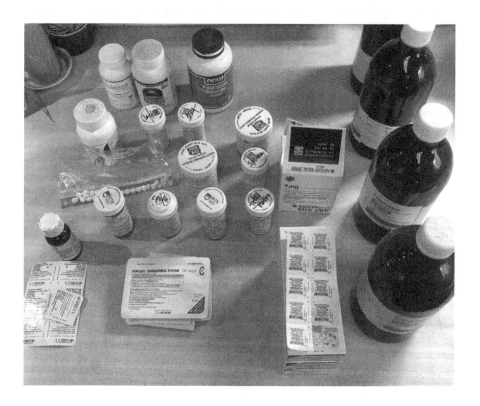

April 9, 9:20 AM

Grief bookends my day. I've posted about Amy's shirt that hangs on the door to the den where she lived[70] (I wanted to call it her lair, but she said that made her feel like a monster in the bad sense, something she already struggled with feeling like). I start and end each day with that shirt, feeling it,[71] pressing it to my face, using it to call up the pain I know is there, to make sure I take the time – if even just twice a day – to feel it and let it out.

Then once the pain has welled up, I collapse into her recliner and sob. There's a lot to sob about, and the exact thoughts vary each time. Like I posted about, having this opportunity to fully pursue my dream is a mixed blessing. I can't stand going anywhere near the suggestion that Amy's death was in any way a good thing.

A couple days ago I was sobbing that something fantastically good had better come out of losing her, and that thought came back in this new context. So I said that this opportunity is a good start, but as always I had to be clear that nothing will ever turn her death into a good thing.

"Think of it as compensation," replied the Amy-voice, and I burst out laughing, laughing for a good minute. Fair enough. I can work with that.

---

70 March 7, 9:51 PM
71 April 28, 11:12 AM

Reflections: This experience set me on the path to accepting that, since there is no going back – there is no reversing what's happened – then there is no shame in feeling joy at something good, even if it only comes as a consequence of her death. In fact, given that she died and I can't undo that, how much better that something marvelous should come out of it!

April 9, 5:51 PM

Merlin does have a condition that requires mild medication, but that's not why I'm posting this. The last word in the note is "Wabu!"

Wabu is our affectionate shorthand for "I love you". I give Amy credit for inventing it early on; as I recall it developed from "I wuv you".

Because it's short and goofy, we only used it for casual situations like notes – "I love you" was still what we said when that's what we wanted to communicate in a meaningful way or moment. But wabu was a handy word that was fun to say and captured the goofiness that was a core piece of our bond.

In addition to using it to close out notes, short emails, voicemails, etc., it's what we said whenever... so, like I've said, Amy lived downstairs for the past five years. And even though I've been home for work for that whole time, she still could feel lonely with me upstairs for hours at a time. So whenever I went downstairs, for any reason quick or not, I'd at least pop my head into the doorway of the den to say Hi – except what I said was mostly just "wabu!" If we had something to talk about while I was there, wabu was how we closed it out.

I never thought about it before, but having this casual way to say we loved each other meant that we said we loved each other a lot more often than we would've if we had to say "I love you", with all its weight.

Reflections: Oh, how I want to hear Amy say "wabu!" again. It's those unique expressions and behaviors that no one is ever going to do again that I miss the most. Of course, I could introduce them with someone else at some point in the future ... Last time that occurred to me as a possibility, it felt horribly wrong, like I'd be somehow trying to recreate my relationship with Amy, or replace her, or something weird like that. But apparently I've been healing, because now it doesn't necessarily feel like a bad idea. My feelings aside, there's no inherent reason an expression like "wabu" has to be specific to Amy and me. In fact, might it not be better to keep it alive? It doesn't have to be just a memory, and if I find at some point in the future that the thought of it doesn't hurt, using it with someone else could be a way of honoring that creative way Amy and I found to express our love. Put another way, if they mean that much, I might be better off looking for ways to keep these things alive than to put them on some mental shelf to gather mental dust.

April 10, 8:43 AM

I'm not a British royal follower at all, but on a simple human level, this statement got me crying for the Queen's loss. As devastated as I am to have lost Amy after eight years, I can't imagine it when you've been with the person for 73 years.

The Royal Family [Twitter post]

@RoyalFamily

"He has, quite simply, been my strength and stay all these years, and I, and his whole family, and this and many other countries, owe him a debt greater than he would ever claim, or we shall ever know. –Her Majesty The Queen, 1997[72]

---

72 https://twitter.com/RoyalFamily/status/1380815077914382338

April 11, 9:35 PM

Here's a classic Amy story involving Stanley Kubrick's right-hand man, Leon Vitali, on the left below (I'm pretending to pick Amy's pocket for the photo).

We were at the Austin Film Festival in 2015, and attended a special 50th[73] anniversary screening of *The Shining*, which was to have a Q&A afterward featuring Leon – who we knew little (Amy) to nothing (me) about.

We got there early and sat down. A few minutes later, a small group sat in the same row a few seats down. Amy decided that one of them looked like an interesting character, so she got up and went over to meet him.

It was Leon, and they got along well (as you can see). We caught up with him after the Q&A as he was smoking, and ended up wandering up and down Sixth Street – and it was Halloween, so the street was jammed with people in costume or not.

---

73 Oops, make that 35th!

They drank a couple beers along the way, and were quickly holding onto each other to stay upright. I followed along, and Amy kind of forgot I was there.

She emailed him when we got home, and while he never replied and she never bugged him, when he came to Portland for a special screening of another Kubrick film, we went up to the stage to say Hi afterward, and he not only remembered Amy, but remembered enough of what she told him about her health to ask how she was in a genuine way.

She had a knack for meeting celebrities, and never seemed to run out of stories.

Reflections: This memory holds the usual mix of feelings for me. I'd never have done what Amy did, so I'd never have met this gracious, engaging person without her, much less had an unforgettable experience with him. But the way she focused on him and ignored me was, of course, painful – and driven by alcohol, since she never behaved that way sober. In the long run, I can choose to use her boldness as an inspiration to take more risks socially.

April 12, 4:29 PM

Here's a poem Amy wrote near the end of her Air Force service, when she'd already been transferred from Japan to CA due to her eating disorder, and still wasn't able to get it under control.

Her relationship with her body took an enormous toll, and I suspect it was one of the reasons she usually had to drink a lot to socialize. She didn't talk about it much, but after the sepsis in 2015, she gained a lot of weight, and even though she couldn't eat much in the last five years, she kept gaining – in part, no doubt, from the 5000+ calories of wine she was drinking every day. Such a vicious cycle! I never did figure out how to help her with that.

> REQUIEM a la FEMME FAT, et al
> May 1999
>
> Rest in peace
> Herculean ooze
> Ample, cushioning, corpulent curves
> Insular and isolate
> Go with God
> Adipose adversary
> Pouting, sagging, dimpled pox
> Born chubby chastity
> Here lies fat
> Gargantuan girth
> Inert, pitted, weighty pudge
> Soft somatic sorrow

Reflections: In case it's not obvious, the title contains a pun on "femme fatale," and is no doubt a reference in her mind to her relationship to attractiveness. Being thin should've made her feel attractive, but it didn't, despite the clear fact that as she'd lost her childhood weight, she had, in fact, attracted more people. All she could see in her body was the shadow of the "weighty pudge" that she'd carried as an adolescent – her lifelong "adipose adversary." At this time in her life, she weighed less than 100 pounds, sometimes as little as 90, so on the face of it, writing a requiem to that fat she'd shed would be appropriate, yet she never felt like she got rid of it. It was a dark period in her life, and this poem captures a lot of the bitterness that occupied her then.

April 13, 7:19 AM

Nabemono (Japanese hot
pot) was one of Amy's
favorite special meals to
make – and perhaps the one
I'm least likely ever to tackle.

It really is a fun group meal,
adding the mushrooms,
seafood, veggies, tofu –
whatever you want, really –
to the broth.

And I have all this kit for it,
but it's so unfamiliar, and
of course I could choose to
learn, but I already have a lot
of that to do that's more important to me.

Anyone want it?

Reflections: This is an example of a decision I made too soon. It was a mistake to think I was ready to get rid of something so meaningful, so Amy-laden. Happily, a friend told me nabemono is fairly easy, and that encouraged me to keep it all.

April 14, 11:49 AM

The demands of my job, three dogs, cooking for myself, maintaining a house, and upkeep on a third of an acre, all conspire to make it easy for me to forget that I'm still grieving.

It's an approximation, I suppose, of what my life will someday be like – when this initial period of intense mourning has passed and I've reached a new equilibrium. A "new normal".

Except that, at the moment, the idea of it ever being normal that Amy's gone is terrifying and painful, and my heart cries out that it can never be so. Acceptance is a ways off! I suspect the suddenness of her death – the fact that I only had twelve hours, one night, to start to adjust to the possibility that she might die, before she actually was dying – is a big part of this.

But I also think new grief tends to pile on layers of previous grief... more on that later.

Reflections: I have reached a new normal now, and it does closely resemble what I describe in this post. The key difference is that instead of a job with defined hours working for someone else, I'm writing this book at my own pace, and can stop and cry whenever I need to. I never for a moment lose sight of what a rare privilege this is, not having to stuff down my grief in order to function for someone else so I can eat and pay my bills.

April 15, 7:59 AM

I've talked a lot here about the different things Amy suffered from, physically and emotionally.[74] There were periods of time when she was mostly able to enjoy our life, but there were also plenty of times when she couldn't go to the musical we had tickets to, or she wasn't up for meeting friends for dinner, or we went down to the Bay Area Maker Faire but she had to stay in the hotel room for a day, or she'd say she wanted to clean the house but wasn't up for doing much of it, so I did it.

When we got together, she'd been sick enough for long enough that she had an official disabled parking placard. Despite C.diff. infections and sepsis and a DVT[75] and raging GERD[76] and so much more that she went through after that, her average level of health was higher during the time we had together – I'm sure a significant part of that came from the emotional boost she got from being with me.

But for me, it was agonizing to see her go through all that, to be so often in pain and discomfort and be so unable to help much. After the sepsis, I never quite kicked the habit of making sure she was still breathing when I found her asleep. Perhaps the worst part of all of it was that she rarely told me what she was dealing with, no matter how I begged her.

---

74 February 11, 7:32 AM

75 Deep vein thrombosis

76 Gastroesophogeal reflux disease

It's becoming clear that I had no idea how profoundly that was affecting me, since I had to stay strong and functional for her. The amount of relief I feel that she's no longer suffering is overwhelming, and I'm sure a lot of that is actually relief for myself, no longer having to suffer for her suffering.

Reflections: Oof, that last line … such honesty. I think I remember getting to the end of the post, starting the last sentence, and then having the thought that maybe some of what I was feeling was about me. I'd much rather not think about the degree to which feelings I think of as caring about Amy are actually about myself, but somehow this time I managed to do it.

April 15, 10:19 AM

Well, this is gut-wrenching... not only did I just realize that Corgi Beach Day is the same weekend as the Willamette Writers Conference – I've already made plans to take B and her girlfriend to CBD – but now I discover that the Alanis Morissette/Garbage/Liz Phair concert Amy and I have tickets for is ALSO that weekend.

I can live with only doing the conference on Sunday. And CBD clearly takes precedence over the concert, but I hate having to give up an Amy-related event AND one I'd love to go to even without that factor.

Well, more grieving to do. The concert is Sat., Jul. 31 at 7:00 PM, in Ridgefield, WA at the Sunlight Supply Amphitheater. Who wants two tickets?

Reflections: I've since realized that while "grieving" is a fine word, it's also a broad word, and what I'm really talking about here is letting go. In particular, letting go of the feeling that I'd somehow be disappointing Amy if I didn't go to Corgi Beach Day.

April 15, 1:40 PM

My earlier post about the concert was prompted by listening to my Alanis playlist. The fact that some of her songs make me cry has always been a good thing. But this song, "Torch," I wasn't expecting and it hit me like a wall of grief. It's about, of course, a breakup, but applies to any form of loss. Here's how it starts:

> I miss your smell and your style and your pure abiding way.
> Miss your approach to life and your body in my bed.
> Miss your take on anything and the music you would play.
> Miss cracking up and wrestling and our debriefs at end of day.
> These are things that I miss.
> These are not times for the weak of heart.
> These are the days of raw despondence.
> I never dreamed I would have to lay down my torch for you like
>   this.

Reflections: I'd guess my days of raw despondence lasted maybe a month? But the memory of them – feeling like everything within fifty miles reminded me that My Love was dead, feeling no pleasure in even my most favorite things – will never leave me.

April 16, 8:04 AM

Another re-evaluation... like most of us, I've had beliefs about what makes for a strong relationship. I've never put much stock in commonalities, believing that factors like the ability to work through conflict are much more important.

But if I measure my relationship with Amy the way I'm used to doing, it was a crappy one – and I had doubts, as I've mentioned.

We could rarely manage to discuss something meaningful without it turning into an argument. Neither of us felt safe sharing what we were dealing with. We both carried resentments toward the other that we couldn't constructively talk about. Neither of us was able to show our love as much as we wanted to. And so on – there's a lot more.

And yet. What I see now is two people, with a solid bond based on commonalities of childhood and youth experience that meant much more than I ever guessed, who met deep needs neither of us were really aware we had. And that was enough.

Every relationship is unique because the people involved are unique, so it stands to reason that using one set of predetermined standards to measure every relationship is problematic. Or put another way, there may be as many ways of making a relationship work as there are relationships.

Reflections: By "commonalities" I mean "oh, we like the same bands" or "hey, we both went to church as kids." But maybe it's more meaningful to think about shared experiences. Amy and I both had childhoods with religious experiences that we came to see as extreme; we each had some idea what the other went through. We shared appreciation for classical music, not because of a happenstance of musical taste, but because we were both raised with it. Being only five months apart in age meant we'd experienced the same things in the world at the same points in our development. Those are shared experiences that gave us common ground that was fundamentally meaningful in a way mere commonality isn't.

April 17, 9:07 AM

The New Yorker is a serious magazine for the most part, but they fit in some humor, most notably in the cartoons that pepper each issue. Here is my favorite so far this year.[77]

"Goodbye, Rascal. You were truly an enormous hampster."

Zachary Kanin / The New Yorker Collection / The Cartoon Bank

Once upon a time, Amy would share with me cartoons she liked, and cut out the ones she loved, to put on the fridge or tape to her computer monitor. She would even read entire articles to me. I don't recall what I thought of that at the time, but now I treasure those memories because they represented Amy letting me into her inner world in a way she rarely did.

---

77 February 16, 9:42 PM / March 14, 11:50 AM

It's been several years since she did any of that – one more sign of a gradual change in her that I've had a hard time finding the right words for... like an atrophying process, perhaps, a slow loss of behaviors that once seemed very much a part of her. I'm open to the possibility that I'm imagining it, trying too hard to extract meaning and patterns in our life together, desperate to understand her. But it did feel like I was, in some way slowly losing her even while she was alive.

There were also positive changes in recent years, some enabled by her cutting back on drinking, which let more of her personality out. The more she drank, the less herself she seemed. I could be forgetting, but it feels like she made me laugh more last year than any previous year. I know we'd have laughed together over this cartoon.

April 17, 4:16 PM

Grocery shopping is another activity I now have a complex relationship with.

In the beginning, Amy and I went together, and we had fun with it. She loved it because she'd always had to do it alone. Then for a while after the sepsis she wasn't well enough for it, so I went alone. I think there was a period in which she sometimes joined me, but several years ago it settled into something I did. She'd write the list, I'd ask questions to make sure I understood what she wanted, then almost inevitably I'd text from the store with more questions – I'm sure a lot of you are familiar with that process. I never stopped missing her company, even though the last times she joined me she was more annoyed with me than enjoying it.

Even with all the questions and texting, I still brought home the wrong thing, more often than I was happy about. Misunderstandings would certainly account for some of that, and occasionally I'd forget something she told me but I didn't write down. But there was another factor: inevitable drift between Amy's knowledge of the store and what they actually carried. And she rarely believed me when I said they didn't have the thing she wanted. I took to keeping the shopping lists around for a week in case there were questions.

It was a source of tension and unhappiness, as I brought in the bags when I got back, and waited to see if anything was wrong. Much of this past year she even stopped participating in putting it all away. She said I could leave it for her, but that never felt right to me.

I miss it all. The first several times I went to the store after she died, I had tears in my eyes the whole time. I'd have been alone anyway, but I wanted all the context back. I want the worry about getting the right thing, I want the texting and the frustrated replies. I want the cries of annoyance as she discovered the wrong or missing thing.

I want there to be a reason for me to text, when I get into the car with the groceries, "All done, my love."

Reflections: I think the first several times I went grocery shopping, I did mutter out loud "all done, my love" when I started the car afterward. I can still cry thinking of it – the power of those little rituals.

April 18, 10:39 AM

I have a journey ahead of me, deciding what my relationship will be with the substance that killed my Amy.

Here is the note she put on the box of wine in the fridge on the first Monday in January. She knew she was getting sick again, with alcoholic hepatitis, as had happened in September. This note, with its smiley face, is so Amy, and I loved her for it. I was so hopeful that she'd quit and done it with a sense of humor.

Somehow – I still don't understand it – even after nine days without alcohol, her liver and kidneys still gave out the next week, suddenly, overnight.

Of course it's not alcohol's fault that Amy chose it for her substance addiction. Drugs certainly held no appeal to her; she always got off prescription opioids as soon as she could after hospitalizations.

I've never been much of a drinker, in part because I don't like the taste of fermentation or the smell of hops, and in part from a deep-rooted aversion to surrendering control of myself to something else, and in part because I don't enjoy the behavior of drunken people. I did discover I like some sweet liqueurs.

But with Amy I started drinking wine, a glass with meals when she wanted me to have one. I'm sure she wanted that because it made her feel a bit less like a lush (a word she once called herself) to have me drinking with her. I never really enjoyed it because few wines are sweet enough for me and I dislike tartness.

So I still have the Bailey's and the Amaretto I put in my hot chocolate once or twice a week over winter. I haven't touched them. And I still have what's in the liquor cabinet Amy left behind – the port, rum, sherry, etc. I'm in no hurry to deal with that.

I figure at some point in my healing process my mind will naturally figure it out. I'm sure I'll feel a pull to have a glass of wine here or there to honor Amy. But my previous aversion to alcohol is at least as strong now, if not stronger.

Reflections: The phrase "the substance that killed my Amy" is a strong one, for sure, and some of my friends got defensive about it. It reflects how I felt at the time. There's a fair argument that the disease of alcoholism killed her, because it's what kept her drinking too much, yet the deadly, terminal effects on her body were directly the result of the alcohol itself. And there's a growing body of scientific evidence that any amount of alcohol consumption is bad for us.[78] For every person who clearly drinks themselves to death, there are likely many more whose deaths come earlier than they would have, due to alcohol, or whose elder years are not as vibrant or energetic due to the accumulated effects of alcohol. I don't judge anyone for what they do to get through life – I just want everyone to live long, healthy lives.

[78] *May 20, 6:46 AM*

April 19, 6:55 AM

So I come downstairs this morning. I walk through to living room toward the den, Amy's lair, to do my ritual sobbing that starts the day.[79]

I see the dog toys scattered around, and laugh, enjoying the feeling that someone else lives here.

Then I think how Amy would've put them all away the previous night, and I cry because she's not here to do that.

I feel a bit odd that I have yet to have the experience so many people seem to, of catching myself thinking Amy's still here. I've been utterly aware for every moment of the last three months that she's gone. Not judging myself – it's just curious.

---

79 March 7, 9:51 PM

Reflections: I'm talking about moments like "Oh, I've gotta tell _____ about this," then remembering the person is gone. It seems to be a common one, yet it's rarely happened to me. I don't know what to make of that!

April 20, 6:03 PM

Anyone want a lightly used treadmill?

I kind of hate this thing.

I think we got it around two years ago, though that's hard to believe. Amy wanted to get moving more, and although she'd occasionally say she wanted to go on walks with me, whenever I asked her, she said no. I couldn't really ask her about those kinds of decisions because she almost always just got defensive or evasive. In this case, my guess is she didn't want people to see her, since she hated her body.

In order to fit it where it is, we had to get rid of the lovely mid-50s Yamaha piano we'd gotten for B. And move an entire ceiling-height bookshelf. Well, I say "we", but I did most of the work.

But she did use the treadmill initially, for at least a week. I know because the office is right above the den, so I could hear it. Strangely, when I mentioned in passing that I could hear it, I never heard it again, or saw her using it, or saw any sign she was using it.

She'd say she was using it, but she had a tendency to exaggerate things she wanted to be true, probably to avoid feeling bad about them not being true.

So it sat there for a year and a half while she pretended she was using it.

It's not a reminder of anything useful or positive, just a reminder of how little Amy shared with me of what she was going through.

Like I said, anyone want a treadmill? I'll deliver it to the Portland area (or, of course, the Gorge). Long furby not included (her name is Bubbles).

Reflections: Regarding "how little Amy shared with me of what she was going through," I think there was a point, during an argument, when she complained that I never asked her how she was, so I started doing that. Probably not quite every day, but close to it. And I rarely got more than one word in reply. There were aspects of her I understood perhaps better than she did, and then there were aspects like this that I never figured out.

April 21, 5:28 PM

And with that, a two-hour farewell video hangout, my time with Oxalis.io is over.[80]

I didn't expect that the first thing I'd do was burst into tears, but I did. I'm not sure why... the most likely reason is that it feels Amy-related, maybe because this is the job I had when she was still around? Not that I really need to know exactly why or what I'm grieving.

I've been excited for the past two weeks, looking forward to managing my time all as I see fit. Thankfully I'm a (perhaps overly) productive person who doesn't need external structure to get done either what needs to get done or what I want to get done. But jettisoning the requirement of having to work during certain hours and feeling guilty if I take care of any life business - that's a huge relief.

At the same time, my sleep has been crappy this past week, and there's no obvious reason. Sometimes I bury my worry, so it's possible I'm carrying more fear about this new chapter of my life than I can see. It could also be a byproduct of how hard I've been working to wrap up so I don't leave untidy loose ends for others to deal with.

To use my favorite catchphrase from the last Narnia book, Onward and Upward!

---

80   April 7, 5:27 PM

Reflections: "jettisoning the requirement of having to work during certain hours" – turns out that habit dies hard! It took me months to start to let go of feeling like I should be working at 9am, and it only recently occurred to me that I don't have to wait till after 4 (when my work day ended) to pick up the mail from the PO box.

April 21, 8:52 AM

Well, I made it into the second episode of *The Muppet Show* before stopping to bawl. I wanted something to relax to, and that seemed perfect, and I was enjoying myself, and I even made it past the first time I thought how much Amy would've loved it with me.

I've mentioned Amy's love for the The Muppets.[81] She'd do Miss Piggy saying "Kermy", she'd sing the musical theme to NPR's *Weekend Edition* as Beaker, and we'd both do the Swedish Chef together.

And it caught up to me. Because while I can enjoy the show, and I can enjoy it with Amy in mind, and imagine her enjoying it, the fact is that I don't want to do any of that. I want to enjoy it *with* her – to hear her laughing, to look over and see the joy on her face, to say "bork, bork, bork" at the same time.

I'm trying, but it's just not the same, and it's never going to be the same, and I can't imagine ever enjoying the show as much with anyone else as I would've with her. So I'm grieving not only that I can't watch it with her, but that I never got to watch it with her in the first place - oh, how I'd love to have memories of that.

Okay. Back to the show. I will keep trying, trusting that some day the enjoyment will be pure and that the Muppet connection Amy and I had will just add to the pleasure.

---

81 February 21, 10:01 AM

April 22, 9:55 AM

A follow-up thought on this post[82] from early February... as a strong general rule, I find crying to be a healing activity, not just for emotional trauma but for physical trauma as well. (Amy had an aversion to crying, feeling like it wasn't useful, and that was heartbreaking for me.)

But it's possible for crying not to contribute to healing, and the key seems to be maintaining *some* sense that the feeling I'm crying over isn't literally true. If I lose all sense of what reality is, and I'm entirely inside the trauma, then it's more like I'm just reliving it. The healing seems to come from hanging on to even a sliver of reality, to contradict the message that the feeling is true.

So as I entered my fourth month of grieving Amy, I began to get the sense that I might be settling into the trauma of losing her, and needed to boost my connection to reality. I find that humor is usually a good way to do that, and my inner Amy-voice has been helpful (of course!).

As I cry and let the thoughts and feelings come up and out, I mix in saying things like this out loud: "Someday, I'll be happy without you. Whether I like it or not." That's my favorite one at the moment because the second part makes me laugh (my Amy-voice added it). And then cry, which is perfect.

---

82 February 5, 8:54 AM

Reflections: I'd lost track of "Someday, I'll be happy without you. Whether I like it or not." I still find it pretty funny! I like the idea that the healing path I'm on will lead me inexorably to happiness.

April 22, 3:46 PM

I'm still stumbling over language sometimes. I already mentioned the choice between I/my and we/our,[83] which sometimes trips me up. I think I just need to default to we/our and accept that for now.

But that's not the only one. I was getting my hair cut, and there was a basket of products on the counter. I recognized one of them because I'd just noticed it under the kitchen sink – that's where Amy washed her hair.

And I started to think, hey, that's the same one Amy —

But "the same one Amy had" is wrong because that sounds like the product isn't here, while "the same one Amy has" is wrong because that sounds like Amy's still here. So I have to stop and think in order to come up with something like "the same one Amy was using".

---

83   January 21, 10:30 PM

Reflections: I still feel self-conscious that this kind of thing trips me up. I have no idea how many other people struggle with it, and I know my brain is particular about language, so I suspect the answer might be "not many." I am finally starting to see that it doesn't really matter to anyone else how I handle those situations, and that will help me let go of this sense that there's a right way to do it.

April 23, 8:43 AM

Apparently, somehow, today marks 100 days since Amy died. Time has been passing much faster for me than it has in a long time, which is disturbing. But that's a topic for another time. I still don't feel any closer to accepting her loss, but that's also a topic for another time.

100 days seems like a nice round number on which to announce that I plan to turn these posts into a book. The seed was planted when Johan and Judy mentioned they could see my posts being a book that counselors would use. And the thing is, y'all keep telling me, in various ways – sometimes through tears – how meaningful this stuff is to you.

All I wanted to do when I started was help us talk about death more, something we don't do much of in our culture. It didn't occur to me that just being honest about my grief would have value. But I figure, if this many people out of my maybe 200 active Facebook friends find it meaningful, then getting it out to a larger audience could help a lot of people.

And that's obviously a good thing in itself. But what really pushes me is that I want something good to come out of Amy's death. The idea of us being a team working from both sides of the grave to help people – I want that rather deeply.

My idea is to use the posts verbatim, with additional commentary since there's usually stuff I can't reasonably fit into each post. Since I already assembled the first three weeks' posts into a file, I'm going to try this approach with that and see if the commentary adds to the value.

Stay tuned!

Reflections: It took me a couple months of processing to come to this decision. One influential thought was that I tend to learn much more from reading specific examples than from reading general observations, so it makes sense that simply presenting my posts, with their context-specific thoughts about my specific grief, could provide some value. Ultimately, though, it's the degree to which all kinds of people — some I haven't seen or talked to since high school — went out of their way to tell me my posts were meaningful or useful or helpful to them, that pushed me to bookify what I was posting.

April 24, 1:16 PM

Well, it's gone.[84] And boy did that
hit me hard – not for what it is, but
for what it represents. Why did she
stop using it? Was she self-conscious
about me being able to hear her using
it? Was there some physical limitation
I didn't know about that got in the
way? So many of Amy's choices and
behaviors I'll never understand.

And it doesn't stop there. It breaks
my heart that she didn't talk to me
about so much of what she was going
through, and that she had so little
attention for what I was going through
(I don't ever remember her asking
me how I was, how I was doing, etc.).
I hate feeling like we were living
separate emotional lives.

I haven't cried that hard in a month.

---

84 April 20, 6:03 PM

Reflections: I think I'm in the process of letting that feeling go, as part of choosing to focus on the positive, meaningful aspects of my relationship to and time with Amy. I can't change Amy's death, so the choice I do have is to keep dwelling on all the unhappiness I carried around, or to acknowledge it, then let it go and celebrate all the joy and love we found together.

April 24, 3:22 PM

This is the permanent niche cover for Amy's spot at Willamette National Cemetery.[85] I had a much longer inscription in mind, but you don't get much space at all, something like 22 characters.

"Peace and Corgi Love" is part of the title of one of her pieces in *The Hood River News*,[86] and it means a lot to me to have her own words here – plus, of course, they represent her pretty well.

---

85 March 4, 6:56 PM

86 The full text of Amy's article, "Why we do this: 'A dose of peace and Corgi love,'" can be found in the appendix.

Reflections: The first time I started to refer to this spot as where Amy was, a voice reminded me that her body wasn't her; in addition, her body isn't there either. So unlike all the scenes in movies and episodes of shows, you'll never find me going there to talk to her. I get that the trope is a convenient narrative shorthand, but I suspect we who have lost loved ones have a much wider variety of places where we feel we can talk to our dearly departeds.

April 25, 3:58 PM

Amy and I were both "on" people who had trouble relaxing, at least internally. We could sit still for hours, in a relaxing setting, but internally we were always busy. And for me it also manifests in always being productive and efficient with my time. Even the way I open and close screw-top bottles is in the most efficient way.

I think the fact that I shared that basic pull with Amy was useful, since she'd've been perennially frustrated with me if I'd gone about things in a measured, relaxed way.

That characteristic of mine came in handy this past week, which was crazy full of appointments and things I had to do – I was fried by Friday (ha!) but had to keep going. And I got done what I needed to.

But the truth is that, while being able to go into a productive, efficient mode when it's called for is useful, it's become clear to me that being in this mode non-stop is bad for me. Specifically, bad for my sleep, which has a host of cascading consequences for my physical and mental health.

So as I emerge from and recover from Hellweek, I am determined to change. I don't actually think it's so much about how *much* I get done in a day, as it is about *how* I get it done. I just want to relax and slow down as I do what I do. And I want to prioritize my sanity over my desire to get as much done in a day as possible.

In addition, as I enter this new phase of life in which one key to my success will be my creative output, I think sleep – and the brain benefits it brings – will be more important than ever.

Reflections: I've made progress with this. When I look at my to-do list for the day, my question is, "How much of this can I realistically get done without stressing myself out?" Then if necessary, I bump items to another day. "Hellweek" is just a characterization of the crazy previous week I described.

April 25, 9:15 PM

For the most part I was able to enjoy my first Oscars without Amy.

The one time I lost it was when Glenn Close not only recognized the E.U. song "Da Butt" from the movie *College Daze*, but knew some of the backstory AND got up and did a bit of the dance.

I'm not familiar with the movie or the song, but there's a good chance Amy was – and either way, I didn't get to see her reaction to that remarkable Glenn Close moment. I wanted to see her hoot and holler and grab her phone to check out the inevitable internet frenzy.

She'd have eaten it all up. And, of course, even if I'd watched the Oscars before her, I wouldn't have seen most of the movies. Now I have, and it's all thanks to her.[87]

---

87 March 30, 5:25PM

April 26, 12:07 PM

Here's another confusing experience... back when we lived in Hood River, I'd take B to a paint-it-yourself pottery shop. I mostly did little critters like this to put in with Amy's houseplants, and they've been there ever since.

So now every time I water the plants – which I've been the sole one to do for several years now, like so many chores – I'm looking at things I made for Amy out of love for her and to enhance her enjoyment of something she loved (her plants were important to her), but now they're just mine.

At the moment, it's hard to get the same pleasure out of them as I did when they were my gifts to her.

Reflections: The "now they're just mine" part is still painful, but I do like them, and I'm getting closer to enjoying their Amy association. I certainly wouldn't want to get rid of them, and if I imagine, say, putting them in a box somewhere, that sounds sad. The pots would seem empty without them, so I guess I've chosen the path of reclaiming them for myself.

April 27, 11:11 AM

This is the article I mentioned as the source of the inscription on Amy's burial niche cover.[88] It's a beautiful reflection of her activist spirit that makes me cry now.

Why we do this: 'A dose of peace and Corgi love'

---

88   The full text of Amy's article can be found in the appendix; see also April 24, 3:22 PM.

Reflections: Oh, that voice, that beautiful voice. I still haven't gotten over the fact that it's been silenced, that the world will no more benefit from her writing. To me, this is a tragedy all on its own. After the copious writing she'd done in her twenties, she finally found her voice in her forties, and it feels so wrong that there was such a relatively short time for her to use it – and for the world to benefit from it.

April 27, 5:58 PM

Every time I use the downstairs bathroom, I'm confronted with these. Amy wasn't a huge Star Wars fan, so I don't think this had deep personal meaning for her, but she enjoyed most of the movies. I imagine it was mostly the romantic in her that wanted these.

The extra dimension to this towel exchange comes from the fact that 95% or more of the I-love-yous in our marriage came out of my mouth.

You might've seen my post a couple months ago about Amy's common response to me saying "I love you",[89] which was "why?" But she did sometimes reply "I know", along with "I love you more" and "someone has to". The variability of that reply was one of the few regular indicators I had of how secure or insecure she was feeling.

---

89 January 20, 7:25 AM

April 27, 8:17 PM

Even in death, through words written for Tom Hanks, Mr. Rogers manages to slip right into my heart...

In this scene[90], he asks the reporter interviewing him, "how long have you been married?" The reporter says, "eight years," and Mr. Rogers says, "that's a wonderful accomplishment."

"A BEAUTIFUL DAY IN THE NEIGHBORHOOD," © 2019 Columbia Pictures Industries, Inc. and Tencent Pictures (USA) LLC. All Rights Reserved. Image Courtesy of Sony Pictures Entertainment.

---

90 From the movie *A Beautiful Day in the Neighborhood*

It's still easy for me to focus on how much more time I wanted with Amy, rather than loving the time we had. But it's true, she could've died multiple times, or been much, much sicker. There were points when she'd been so mad and hurt so much that I wouldn't have blamed her if she'd concluded she'd be better off without me.

But she stuck with me, as much as I stuck with her. And we had so much fun, shared so much enjoyment and meaning. And together, in those eight years, we gave B a solid enough life that she could go off into the world – something that was not always a given.

So, yes, "a wonderful accomplishment"... I'm hanging on to that one.

Reflections: I think I can use regular reminders of this. She almost died once in the few months after we reconnected but before we got together. Contemplating that things could always have been worse helps me remember to be grateful for what I did get instead of obsessing over what I didn't get. This is why now, as part of my nightly gratitude prayer,[91] I'm thankful for the life and the health that Amy did get to have.

91 January 24, 11:54 AM

April 28, 11:12 AM

Something new happened yesterday morning, a natural departure from my grieving norm.

I'd finished breakfast and was closing the drapes for my post-breakfast nap, when I realized I'd skipped the grieving ritual I've been doing every morning since Amy died.[92] I didn't go to the door of the den and feel her and feel the loss, and cry.

I felt a flicker of guilt before seeing that this is a sign of healing – and a sign of a more flexible life. While I was working, it was easy to get caught up in Doing and forget to feel, so having that ritual was vital to keeping my grieving process going. Now, I can stop and grieve almost any time I want, and I do that.

Then last night, I went to do my bookend ritual – the same thing just before bed – and I didn't need to cry. I'd cried plenty during the day, so I didn't push it. I just focused on gratitude and love.

This morning I caught myself heading to the kitchen instead of the den, and I thought, "it's okay." I don't need to force it. Maybe tomorrow I'll want the ritual again, or maybe not – so goes the healing.

---

92   March 7, 9:51 PM

Reflections: This shirt is the only item of the clothes Amy was wearing that I haven't washed. It still has her hair on it, and I like that. Posting this made me awkwardly self-aware of the morning ritual for the next several days. I remember coming downstairs and panicking – do I go do the shirt ritual or not? It was hard to let that decision happen naturally, at least for a while, until I was able to let go of it fully. I still do that ritual every night, though it's finally occurred to me that maybe I don't need the shirt to fulfill the meaning of the ritual.

April 29, 11:40 AM

Another of the songs Amy and I loved to sing together is a duet by Johnny
Cash and June Carter, "Don't You Think It's Come Our Time". I think
we did manage to gather up our scattered words of love and make them
rhyme.

[Johnny Cash:]
I have picked wild roses
Far into September.
But I had no one to give the flowers to.
I needed a celebration
A September coronation
And I admitted to myself I needed you.

[June Carter:]
I've watched the gentle winds change
The colors shades of meadows.
    I've seen the dew on flowers that had no name.
But I let my vase stay empty like my lonely empty heart.
Picking flowers for yourself is not the same.

[Chorus:]
[Both:] Don't you think it's come our time to be together.
Let's gather up our scattered words of love and make them rhyme.
[Johnny:] Let's go pick some flowers and fill our empty vases.
[Both:] Don't you think it's come our time.

[Johnny:] Would you take this small bouquet that leaves a
        fragrance on my fingers
And a feeling that your love is close at hand.
[June:] Thank you for the flowers, now let's walk through the
        meadows
Through the brook where our demands caress the sand.

[Chorus]

Reflections: The metaphor of picking up scattered words of love and making them rhyme is beautiful on its own. It gains extra meaning since Amy and I were both writers and lovers of wordplay. "Scattered" to me also reflects the way we went our own ways in life after meeting in college, then came back together. And rhyming involves choosing words with a similarity to each other, like the way we chose to find our similarities and savor them.

April 29, 2:01 PM

Episode 7 of [NBC's musical show *Zoey's Extraordinary Playlist*] was so well-written, and as usual,[93] so nail-on-the-head for me. She tries the entire episode to recapture a memory of stargazing with her late father, to no avail, but ends up creating new memories that still honor her original experience.

I've mentioned that Valentine's Day and our anniversary were two times Amy and I often stayed at the Edgefield Hotel,[94] and I tried both times to do that. The first time was foiled by Covid and weather, and the second time was foiled by EVERYONE else being there, and by kitchen problems. It was hard to bear.

I'm going to have to write to this show to tell them how well I think they're handling grief, and how much these episodes mean to me. Zoey may not get to sob much, but I sure do.

---

93 February 20, 1:35 PM
94 February 4, 11:31 AM / March 31, 2:46 PM

April 30, 8:29 AM

1998-99 was the darkest time in Amy's life. Her husband had beaten her, her marriage was ending, and she'd been reassigned from Japan to California due to her worsening eating disorder – which represented the one thing she'd encountered that she couldn't master: herself.

It was also the most productive writing period of her life, undoubtedly because she felt she had few people she could share her pain with. The tone of her letters, poems, and stories is bleak and bitter and hopeless and unlike anything before or after.

I can say "unlike anything after" because there was an after. Somehow, in crawling back to Portland after her honorable discharge for PTSD and bulimia, Amy found a way forward, a way toward peace and love. Anyone who knew the fullness of what she'd been through would've completely understood if she'd turned into a horrible wreck of a person. But she didn't.

The irony that hit me yesterday is, the woman who worked so passionately for peace and love found those two things elusive. She may – or may not – have had moments when her inner maelstrom calmed for a bit, but her overwhelming experience of life was anxiety, worry, fear, self-hatred, etc.

And similarly, love was something she felt unworthy of, and felt unable to express the way she wanted.

It's easy to spread peace and love in the world when you feel them. To do so when you don't – that's heroic. And Amy was my hero.

Reflections: "Hero" was a word Amy used often, to characterize a set of behaviors she found desirable, mostly in men. She'd say "my hero" to me sometimes, or "what a hero" to describe someone else. I managed at least once to say to her an abbreviated version of this post, ending with "you're my hero." She stopped writing abruptly when she left the Air Force, so I have little sense for how exactly she recovered her emotional equilibrium in Portland and found a way out of the darkness. But she did. When she was struggling at Travis Air Force Base, in California, she didn't know that hope lay waiting for her. But it did.

May 1, 9:57 AM

I've mentioned "love languages" before,[95] the fact that what Amy and
I each did to communicate love to the other, and what communicated
love to each of us, differed. In fact I never thought we were particularly
compatible in that way.

As far as I can tell, Amy primarily communicated love through cooking. It
was her dominant way of taking care of people she cared about. Of course,
her own relationship to food was conflicted. Her senses of smell and taste
were fantastic, which elevated her capacity for enjoying the act of eating,
yet her eating disorder made the consequences of eating intolerable.

I enjoyed Amy's cooking, appreciated the thought she put into it, and
loved her for all of it. But it's not something that I perceive as love. She
did occasionally complain that I never cooked for her, and I thought about
it, but for various reasons never managed to do it. I did take over making
some meals when she was feeling ill. I'd like to think I'd have tried harder
if it'd occurred to me to think of cooking for her as telling her I loved her,
but it didn't.

The only other way Amy seemed to perceive love, that I identified anyway,
was when I took care of things so she didn't have to worry about them.
That was also a challenge, since I've always been a bit scatterbrained.

By far the dominant way I give and perceive love is through affection.
And beyond the first year or so, Amy was rarely affectionate. Being drunk
sometimes made her more affectionate, but naturally that didn't mean as
much to me. I once told her that if I didn't initiate touch with her, a week
could easily go by without us ever having contact. She seemed unhappy at
that idea, and said she'd work on it, but nothing changed.

I think that's a casualty of her anxiety and insecurity. My sense is that
she had to feel fairly safe and secure to have the emotional space to feel
affectionate toward me. And I'm sure being a survivor of domestic abuse
and of sexual violence played a role too.

---

95 March 7, 9:51 PM

But I do think she savored how affectionate I was toward her. It's quite possible that her relationship toward affection didn't actually reflect any innate tendency so much as it did her trauma.

May 1, 2:10 PM

With this being Amy's birthday month, I'll be giving away things of hers that she didn't use or didn't mean much to her, and that I'm not attached to.

These are all journal-type books, lined except for the top one.

Who wants one?

Reflections: I feel more now about having given these away than I did at the time. The Nietzsche one in particular; it was on Amy's desk, and I kind of wish I'd left it there — her desk is a pile of emotional mines I'd rather leave for some time later. But that journal was unused like the others, which points to another reason it's hard to let go of them: she must've aspired to use it, since she kept it on her desk, so there's a mystery I'll never solve. What would she have used it for? Did she have something in mind? Did she get it just before the sepsis, such that it became one of many casualties of that medical saga? All I can do now is let go.

May 1, 4:18 PM

I watched the Kentucky Derby just now, as I would've with Amy. She didn't watch a lot of sports aside from football and the Olympics, but she never missed a Triple Crown race. I have my own soft spot for these races, leftover from reading Black Beauty and other horse books as a kid.

I'd usually be out in the yard, weeding – as I was this time – and she'd make sure I got back inside in time for the race.

I cry more easily in general these days, and the boy inside me who loved rooting for the underdog horse in those childhood books couldn't help himself this time.

The winning horse – who was not the favorite – got a lead early and never lost it, and the trainer said afterward that he never expected the win, giving all the credit to "that little horse". The trainer himself had just become the winningest trainer in the Derby's history, but all he could talk about was the heart and the spirit of the horse. I'm drying my tears now…

Reflections: Maybe Bob Baffert is lying and Medina Spirit was given a steroid before the Derby; the fact that the horse passed all the drug tests before and after the Preakness and didn't come close to winning would suggest he needed a boost to win. But none of that changes my experience, which was based on one more thing I was doing without Amy instead of with her, and something I had a more emotional connection to than I realized.

May 2, 8:55 AM

Well, I did it. I used "I" instead of "we".[96]

Someone in town is looking for a place to keep their tiny trailer when they're not using it. I thought about saying "we have space", and I would've been okay explaining why when they got here and only met me.

I've talked about leaning into my grief, and I decided to use "I" because it forces me to face how much I hate that – and because I think I'm ready to face it.

So I'm still sobbing as I write this. I'm supposed to be part of a "we" for a lot longer, and having to say "I" instead feels like someone screaming "your wife is dead" in my face.

And yet, as agonizing as it is, that is the reality. And I want to keep pushing myself toward it in a way that promotes healing – because the only thing that would be worse than feeling this way now is to bottle it all up and feel like this the rest of my life.

---

96 January 21, 10:30 PM / April 22, 3:46 PM

Reflections: My pronoun struggle is clearly going to take time to resolve. At some point I realized I'm just going to have to give myself endless space to be messy and awkward and inconsistent about it. It's one area where, on top of any clarity I get as I heal, time really does make a difference – the more time I've had as just me, the more it makes sense to talk about me instead of us.

May 2, 1:38 PM

This hospital sticker has been sitting in the car since January. It's not even from Amy's last day – it's from the last day I had with her, that Monday when I was at the hospital for five or six hours.

She was pretty gorked out on meds ($12K+ in pharmacy charges in three days!) and drifted in and out of consciousness. She couldn't even stay awake to hear all of what the doctors had to say.

But she did ask me to bring her some usual things, like her glasses, computer, etc. I love that she wanted them, because that day she barely managed to use her phone, and didn't seem to have touched it at all after that. She was planning to get better.

I was eager to leave around 3pm to avoid the worst of Portland rush hour traffic, and since we were barely interacting anyway, I didn't feel like I'd miss much. And of course, the next time I saw her, it was her last hour of life.

So this sticker is a potent symbol for me. I'm starting a collection of Amy-related items I want to keep for their symbolic value, and I think this belongs in it.

Reflections: A potent symbol indeed! It took me another month or more to remove the sticker from the car. My memories of – and feelings about – that Monday and Tuesday before Amy died are still on the raw side.

May 3, 8:48 AM

In May 1999, Amy wrote this in a letter:

> There is a route I drive through cow country that enjoys its own grammar and climate. On one shoulder of the only sustained straight stretch stands a sign, which I have always understood as an imperative:
>
> "SUBJECT TO FLOODING".
> No one thing seems ever to oblige.
> Brevity implies the fill of wet.

Seeing that sign as a command is exactly the kind of thing my mind has long done naturally, without effort, and Amy's is the only other mind I've known that matched mine that way.

It's a normal part of my mental life that I'd never been able to share fully before Amy. I could amuse people by sharing those thoughts, but to have someone who was right there with me on it – and would contribute their own – meant more to me than I ever guessed. This private part of me that felt alone suddenly had a friend.

And of course, my mind keeps doing it even without Amy. File this in the same category as all the shared references we had, the words and quotes and noises we loved even out of their original contexts. My brain still makes the references, but there's no one to get them.

I'm finding the loss of my mindmate (in these areas, anyway) to be particularly excruciating.

Reflections: There are plenty of people – including many of my friends – who'd think the same thing at seeing the sign Amy describes. It's just one example of a whole way of viewing and interacting with the world that Amy and I shared. And even if many of my friends share all of that, they're not here. And they're not Amy. I have, though, reached the point that I'll say out loud the things I'd've said if Amy were here. Doing that gets easier to enjoy thoroughly as time goes on, and there's something about saying them out loud that I like. I think it helps counteract the part of me that might feel like, "Oh well, I guess there's no point to that anymore."

May 4, 3:11 PM

It just occurred to me that I can appreciate the Gorge in different ways than Amy did.

Every time I drive into Hood River, there are a couple places the HR waterfront sports scene is visible from – the windsurfers, kiteboarders, etc. And I've often found myself feeling a pang of guilt as I glance at it, because Amy loved to hang out on the waterfront and watch it all. I'm sure some of that came from her general love of our wind.

But there was undoubtedly a personal, perhaps nostalgic, component as well, flowing from the fact that many of both the staff and the customers for the restaurant she and her ex started in HR come from the outdoor sports crowd. I know she enjoyed talking about all that, like explaining how the surprise formation of a huge sandbar after a flood had provided a solution for the differing needs of the windsurfers and the kiteboarders.

And of course, I don't have that attachment to it all. Yet one of Amy's qualities I treasure the most is the facility she had for truly dwelling in a place, for savoring its uniquenesses. That's something I can aspire to as I figure out what it is that grabs me most about living here, in Amy Country.

Reflections: I have long had the tendency to want to fit more into my life than can actually fit, and to feel stressed as a result. So this pull I feel to do things because Amy would've (or might've) done them is something I have to look at carefully before I act. Getting down to the Hood River waterfront once this summer is enough — I don't have to go a bunch of times for her. I know she wants me to enjoy what I like, not obsess about what she liked.

May 5, 11:44 AM

Once upon a time, Loofah was a term of endearment Amy used for me.[97] It came from one of her tales, something about a Storm Large concert and a shirt Storm was wearing that Amy misread. It has nothing to do with sponges or body-cleaning activities – it's a twist on Lover.

She actually had my email address in her contacts as Loofah rather than my name, but I realized at some point that she'd stopped calling me that, and changed to my name in her contacts.

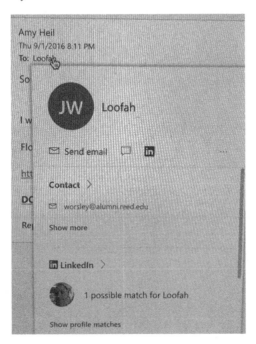

Add the fact that by the end she'd largely stopped using her other pet name for me, John-John, and you have a painful puzzle. As I've mentioned, this isn't the kind of thing I could usually ask her about in any productive way – she'd just get defensive or blow it off.

So I'll never know what was going on. I know she didn't stop loving me, or caring about me, so what was it?

---

97 April 5, 9:33 PM

Reflections: It hurts even more now to have lost those endearing nicknames, since I've also lost the woman who used them. They're just one of many changes in Amy's expression of affection over the years, and enough time has passed that I can choose compassion as my response — compassion for the emotional and physical suffering she endured, that made it hard to be the person she wanted to be.

May 6, 3:14 PM

I think my time with Amy may have let me redeem an unhealthy behavior pattern.

When I was about 2, I took on the job of making my mom happy, something I was obviously incapable of doing at that age. It turned into a lifelong caretaking pattern. Of course, consciously I had no idea when Amy and I got together that she would end up needing so much care – but it can't be a coincidence.

In the face of Amy's insecurities, her neediness, her overwhelming tendency to take everything personally, and more, it became clear to me after several years that I just couldn't make her happy. I had to learn to let go of that urge. I could take care of her, and love her, and show her affection, and try to help keep our life under control so she felt safe, but whether or not all of that added up to her feeling happy or even content – with me or in general – was just out of my control.

It was painful, even agonizing at times, to let go of that. I had to work through feeling like I didn't really care about her because she was unhappy and I wasn't trying to fix it. But she'd done some DBT[98] and other forms of therapy, and had her own ways of working through her feelings. And a world-class ability to just stuff it all down. So she didn't actually need me to fix it.

And as I've posted about,[99] I did, in the end, manage to give her what she needed most. Therein lies the redemption: I go into the relationship desperate to make her happy (based on an old belief that happiness matters most), find that I can't, then learn that being happy wasn't what she really needed and that what she really needed was something I could give her.

I *think* I'm done with the caretaking. Not that I expect to be free from the pull. But I think I finally get now that it doesn't work and distracts me from meeting real needs.

---

98 Dialectical behavior therapy

99 February 5, 4:06 PM

Reflections: In stating "it can't be a coincidence," I neglected to mention that my previous long-term relationship also featured me choosing someone who, in the beginning, was independent but became dependent on me. The development I describe fits on a lifelong timeline, because I can't talk about caretaking without considering related things like being able to take up space, or being able to handle conflict. And in those areas, I had to learn and grow every bit that I did before Amy in order to be the person I was able to be with her. Now in the process of losing Amy and grieving her, I feel my capacity in those areas continuing to grow.

May 7, 5:58 PM

In addition to tracking meals she planned to make,[100] Amy also tracked what was in Jack's Tomb, aka the Jack Freezer, pictured on the right.

It's a separate freezer we got after moving into this house, because we'd end up with so much fruit from our yard to process. Here's the story on the name...

Back then we had a rescue piebald cat named Captain Jack Sparrow.[101] He died one day, out of the blue, while sleeping on the dog food bin, and I was so sad I didn't move him for hours. So he... solidified... in an awkward position.

---

100 January 30, 4:05 PM

101 Yes, after Johnny Depp's character in the *Pirates of the Caribbean* movies.

It was winter, and snowy, so we couldn't bury him, and we decided to, yes, freeze him. Until we figured out what to do. At the time this freezer was in the basement, so I bagged Jack up and stuck him in the freezer, where he stayed well into summer – long enough to warrant naming the freezer. Then we hit upon the idea of a cairn, which we made by the river.

I moved the freezer into the mud room a couple years ago, and it's been slowly emptying. I just made room in our second fridge's freezer for two bags of turkey stock from 2018, which were the last items. Jack's Tomb is now empty, and turned off.

I doubt this'd ever have happened with Amy around, if only because the second fridge's freezer would never've been empty enough for the turkey stock. I did it in order to save money, but it's still one more change to grieve. They just keep coming...

Reflections: Yes, John, changes you choose to make will keep coming as long as you keep choosing to make them ... I'm not making fun of myself. It just amuses me to be able to see now that what I was referring to with "one more change to grieve" was a situation of my own making. Emptying that freezer and turning it off was a good change – it simplified my life a bit, and I was ready to make it.

May 8, 9:06 AM

I think I'm seeing anew how in denial Amy was about the physical effects of her alcohol consumption.

Remember, she was a highly skilled Air Force nurse. She had all the medical knowledge about the bodily damage caused by the toxic byproducts of alcohol, and she'd seen that damage in patients.

Last year, well before her first hospitalization for hepatitis in September, she started experiencing unusual bleeding. She had a small bump on the side of her nose that she had a habit of scratching absentmindedly. Last year it started bleeding a lot when she did that. So did a small bump on her forehead.

I have since learned that this bleeding is consistent with liver damage, but at the time I didn't know that. Her body was trying to tell her to back off the booze, but she just seemed puzzled by it. I don't understand how she didn't make the obvious connection... which has to speak to just how in denial she was.

Reflections: And, of course, there's a part of me that can't help crying out, "If only I'd paid more attention (or something), maybe we could've prevented her death!" I know it's not useful to dwell on that – it's a form of clinging that keeps me from letting go. And the fact is, she'd been unwell for long enough that I'd gotten used to her having minor health issues, and I really can't blame myself for failing to see this bleeding as one of them.

May 9, 8:33 PM

Today has been a hard day. And not just for the obvious reason or two (losing my mom and my wife in the last three years).

Amy played a role in the fact that I didn't get to say goodbye to my mom when she used physician-assisted suicide to escape her aggressive dementia. Mom was an addict who struggled a lot. She lived in my Portland house after I moved in with Amy, then when I sold that house to buy this house, Mom moved to a housing facility that had a 24-hour nurse to help her regulate her many prescription meds (which she was quite capable of using for her own purposes).

But after a while she said it was going downhill – and in fact it had been sold to a huge corporation – so she wanted to move, and decided not to move into another place that would support her as an addict.

Amy had already been uncomfortable with Mom in our life. Mom came to visit sober once or twice, but she mostly showed up high, and above all else Amy felt (naturally) protective of B. The truth is that Amy and I fought a lot over Mom, with Amy wanting to hold a much harder line, and me, well, not (there's so much more to say about all of this!). It was excruciating, feeling like I was having to choose between them.

We were both unhappy about Mom's decision to live without the help she needed, and Amy didn't want her around B any more, so I told Mom she couldn't be part of our life anymore. I wasn't "cutting her out" or anything that extreme – in fact, every day for the next three years, I hoped she would call me, because that would indicate she was healthy.

But she never called, and then I found out she was gone. There's no question that without Amy I'd have handled it all very differently. Of course I have no idea how that would've gone, but I can't help having regrets.

Today, however, I just miss the hell out of both of them. My cheeks have been wet a lot, and I've wailed more deeply than I have in at least a month. I hate that I have to go through this, and for all the words I post here, I can't come close to describing how much it still hurts.

Reflections: None of this absolves me of my role in missing the last several years of my mom's life. As difficult as it would've been for me to make a different choice and go against Amy's way of handling it all, it was still a choice I made. I can't blame myself for making it, but I do want to acknowledge my responsibility for it. "I hate that I have to go through this" represents progress from what I felt earlier, which was various versions of "I don't want this." I was trying to face the fact that whether I want it or not, this is where I am now, and I do have to go through it.

May 10, 4:04 PM

Overflow post from yesterday... here's Amy with the newborn B, who is now an adult in charge of her own presence on the internet, so this seems a good time to tell you her name is Brooklyn.[102] Though Amy did usually refer to her as B, in part due to infant jaundice Brooklyn had, when Amy thought she looked like a bumblebee.

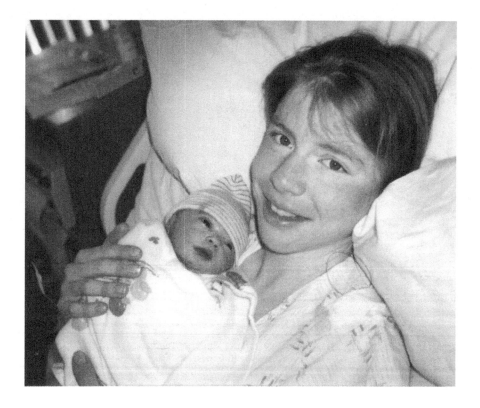

---

102   In keeping with Amy's determination to keep Brooklyn safe on the internet as an adolescent, I'd only ever referred to her as B on Facebook – except for two early posts after Amy's death, when my brain was not tracking everything it normally would. I hadn't even noticed I did that.

Amy'd had two miscarriages before Brooklyn, who was born a month early, and the stress of whose birth cost Amy her spleen shortly afterward. So B was kind of a miracle baby who managed to sneak past the forces that nearly kept Amy childless. That's the look I see in Amy here, a rare moment of vulnerability.

Amy made it clear that B came first and I came second, and called her "my gifted, curious, confident, quantum-minded daughter" as well as "a reminder of both my most cutting sorrow and my greatest joy". She also wrote that "If all else comes to naught, I will have left the world a better place because of her."

When I first met B, I sat down next to her on the couch, where she was playing a game on her Kindle. I'd once been in her situation, where a divorced parent introduces a new adult, so I was open to her having a hard time with it – but B let me right into her world by telling me about the game. She took to me without a second thought, and I've long felt that she could actually be my daughter. This mutual affinity was crucial to how the three of us formed a new family so quickly.

I am grateful beyond words to have Brooklyn in my life.

May 12, 8:43 PM

I've been working a lot on prep for Amy's virtual memorial, which is coming up soon. I aspire to cover the arc of her as a person, not just what she did during her life.

Ironically, I've been grieving less these last two days despite hours of poring over her letters and writings and photos, perhaps because I'm feeling anxious about being ready for the memorial and am in get-it-done mode.

It did just catch up to me a bit. I miss holding hands as we walk to and from restaurants, theaters, and such. I miss how she'd kiss me on the head as I sat at the dining room table playing games with B and friends. I miss coming up behind her as she looked out the window, slipping my arms around her waist, and nestling my head on her shoulder. I miss the awkward way I had to say goodnight, by leaning over her in her recliner, laying my forehead on her shoulder, and snuggling my cheek against hers. I miss trying to hug her in the kitchen and almost invariably being met with irritation.

As Sarah McLachlan put it in my favorite song of hers, *Sweet Surrender*, "I miss everything, everything about you."

Reflections: That awkward goodnight is still high on my list of things I miss, especially feeling my cheek against hers, always so soft ... maybe snuggling my nose into her neck ... in our life so low on physical contact, that moment was an anchor for me every day.

May 13, 9:07 AM

I can't believe it's been five[103] months, gaaah... I wrote before[104] about how I managed to give Amy a space in which she could show the messy, unhappy parts of her. A similar thing may have happened around her achievement-orientedness.

Excellence was expected in her family, and Amy took that drive out into the world, racking up two successful careers by age 42. At that age, when we reconnected, she was so sick she could barely keep food down, required regular potassium infusions to stay alive, and was on unemployment.

Yet she was living on her own, driving herself, etc. She kept that independence until the sepsis in late 2015. After that she never drove again, and resented it when I did things without her. She lived in the recliner in the den, and gradually stopped gardening or even watering the houseplants she loved.

I'll never know exactly what was behind those changes, but I know she struggled with feeling useless. Of course none of it changed how or how much I loved her, and that was hard for her to believe.[105] She'd come to feel from an early age that she had to earn love, and now she wasn't doing any of the things she'd always done to earn that love.

It was so hard for her to accept that I loved her just for who she was. Sometimes I'd playfully poke at that by saying things like, "I love you and there's nothing you can do about it. So there!" It was heartbreaking how unable she was to see how much there was to love about her.

---

103 Four, actually. Tracking time was clearly still a struggle for me at this point.

104 February 12, 10:56 AM

105 February 5, 4:06 PM

May 14, 8:19 AM

On the relatively few occasions I did something without Amy, I liked to
bring her home a gift. Nothing fancy, and usually earrings – like these
on the left, which I think I got at a shop in a small town on Route 116 in
Sonoma Co., CA. Or if I was at a Maker Faire, I'd make her something –
like in the photo on the right.

It took me years to get a sense for the kind of earrings Amy liked, and I
was enjoying my success rate. As I thought yesterday about traveling,
it hit me what a habit it's become to look for gifts for her, and how the
impulse will still come up.

Traveling with Amy could be challenging. She needed to feel like everything was under control, yet she wanted me to handle all the arrangements, which inevitably meant that she got frustrated. But in all her storytelling, when she talked about our trips, it was always with fondness and enjoyment, so I guess the frustration was worth it.

At the time, the rare trip I took without her was refreshing; now, of course, I'll miss her every moment.

Reflections: Buying her earrings meant a lot to me, and she came to anticipate getting them on pretty much every gift-giving occasion. She didn't ask for much by way of presents, and I had to pay attention throughout the year, then make a note whenever she mentioned something she wanted.[106] So in part I liked having something I knew she'd always want. I know she appreciated the fact that I'd figured out what she liked. Mostly, though, the meaning came from having figured out a way to consistently make her happy.

106 *March 14, 11:50 AM*

May 16, 12:50 PM

Brooklyn's first birthday without Amy... you can imagine all the feelings that brings with it.

Mostly I just wish I could – in some hard to articulate way – hit Pause. Time is passing too quickly and I'm afraid of losing or missing things (not the material kind).

Reflections: I don't exactly recall what I had in mind for "afraid of losing or missing things," but it had to do with staying on top of my life. I've long had the fear of forgetting something important, and it does happen sometimes. Trying to manage a life built for two all by myself, with part of my brain function still tied up with grief, has often felt like too much.

May 17, 12:23 PM

I finally found a video with Amy in it[107] – on *her* phone, of all places.

It's from Reed's[108] reunions weekend in 2015, and Amy introduces Brooklyn who goes on to sing Tom Lehrer's song 'The Elements', whose lyrics consist almost entirely of every element in the periodic table that was known at the time.

It's a marvelous moment for B, but for me, there's now at least one place I get to see and hear Amy, and I have no words for how much that means to me.

---

107 March 2, 12:22 PM

108 Reed College in Portland, Oregon, where we met in 1989.

Reflections: I still have no words for how much this means to me, but I'm struck by the fact that Amy seems a bit nervous in the video. Social situations, even in groups, were where she came off the most confident, which is why this stands out to me.

It's endearing, actually. Since I knew how she felt underneath her social masks, I appreciated any hint of vulnerability she showed. Tom Lehrer's music was a pleasure Amy and I had both grown up with, and we loved that B took to this song the way she did.

May 19, 8:58 AM

This napkin has been stored in my desk drawer since I put it there in maybe late 2014, early 2015.

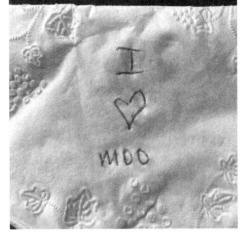

In the beginning, Amy would bring me lunch when I was working from home, and a napkin with a note like this was part of the package. As time went on, she did that less often. I think I kept this one because it'd been months since she brought me lunch, and it was likely the last time.

She wrote "moo" instead of "you" because at the time, B was still in her cow-obsessed phase. As I've mentioned, over time it became rarer for Amy to express her love for me in any overt way, so this napkin is a treasure. *Reaches for a tissue...*

Reflections: It meant a great deal to me that Amy brought me lunch back then. I never asked her to do it, but she'd come upstairs with a tray, always including a napkin with some affectionate message like this. I never understood why she stopped, and I've missed it. Maybe it was classic courting behavior, and at some point she accepted that I was here to stay and she didn't need to go out of her way like that. All I can do now is work to let go of the need to know why, so my appreciation of the memory is unfetteredly a fond one.

May 20, 6:46 AM

"The study replicates previous research that has shown there is no safe limit in the level of alcohol consumption for its role in damage to the structure and function of the human brain."[109]

I sure saw this with Amy. The brain that had once devoured every intellectual challenge, and thrived in a college programming class, now struggled to remember how to DM someone in Instagram.

---

109 *CNN*, "Drinking Any Amount of Alcohol Causes Damage to the Brain, Study Finds," May 19, 2021, https://www.cnn.com/2021/05/19/health/alcohol-brain-health-intl-scli-wellness/index.html.
    From the article: "In an observational study, which has not yet been peer-reviewed, researchers from the University of Oxford studied the relationship between the self-reported alcohol intake of some 25,000 people in the UK, and their brain scans."

Reflections: Knowing how inherently smart she was, it was hard to see Amy struggle with technology. She did suffer from impatience, and got frustrated easily, which didn't help. Being a nurse and an EMT involved plenty of technology, and she'd excelled at it, so it's not like she just had a weakness there. "How to DM someone in Instagram" stands out because B and I showed her how to do it over and over, and she had so much trouble remembering.

May 20, 5:33 PM

This is the first photo of us that I know of. I just found it on her old computer. That look on Amy's face just melts my heart.

Reflections: To have any version of her "I love you" face — you can imagine how much that means. It's not the same when I try to call it up in my head.

May 21, 8:16 AM

Today's random sobfest brought to you by... sneezing.

I felt a tickle in my nose, then a head-voice said "I need to sneeze". I did proceed to sneeze, but those words are Amy's.

She had a curious relationship to sneezing. She'd say "I need to sneeze" because her nose was quite capable of not sneezing for an hour despite a constant tickle.

When she did sneeze, it would usually go on for a while, a dozen or more times. And she'd get annoyed if I said "Gesundheit" beyond the second or third time.

On the other hand, there were also times when she'd sneeze without any warning at all – without the deep intake of breath I need. Just all at once SNEEZE!

And, of course, I miss it all.

May 23, 9:41 AM

I'd forgotten we got this matching set of *Ghostbusters*-themed rings.

It's been years since Amy wore any rings, and mine fell off often enough that it wasn't worth wearing by itself.

I think I'll wear them both now, at least for a while.

Reflections: I do wear them both now, for social situations or cultural events. I keep waiting for someone to ask about them, but the engraving isn't really noticeable unless you're close up. One says "Gate Keeper" and the other says "Key Master," which is a reference to the matching spirits that possess Sigourney Weaver's and Rick Moranis's characters in the movie Ghostbusters. Amy got them for us early on, when feeling romantic about us still came easily for her. Hers had sat in a tiny dish next to the refrigerator all these years, amongst a collection of other rings she stopped wearing, and one day I suddenly had the attention to look at it all.

May 23, 4:28 PM

There's a movie from 2009, *Get Low*, about a guy who wants to have his funeral *before* he dies. I thought of that during Amy's memorial just now, because if she'd been able to see what people thought of her, how much she meant to them, I think it would've made a real crack in the wall of her low self-worth.

I may have said this already, but it bears repeating: we need to learn how to celebrate each other while we're still around.

Reflections: We sometimes do this for public figures in the form of "roasts" and the like. But imagine if this were a normal part of life for the rest of us! I find the idea especially meaningful when applied not to the obvious people who are already recognized as standing out in one or more ways, but to the quiet people, the overlooked.

May 24, 8:58 AM

Another takeaway from Amy's memorial: if there are people you were once friends with, who you fell out of touch with, you can still reach out and rekindle the connection.

If you enjoyed each other then, you likely still will, and your life will be richer for it.

(I write this as much for myself!)

Reflections: This came from seeing how much Amy still meant to people she'd been out of touch with for thirty years. Connections between us are often powerful and lasting, and we don't have to give up on them just because time has passed.

May 26, 8:55 AM

I've decided to attend the Austin Film Festival & Screenwriting Conference. It seems like a good way to confront the fact that I don't get to do these things with Amy, and supports the path I'm on now.

We had a lot of fun at AFF the two times we went, and we both wanted to go back. The truth is also that Amy drank a ton there.

This photo of Amy wearing a replica of the papier mâché head worn by Michael Fassbender's titular character in the 2014 movie *Frank* is still one of my favorite things, and in my phone Amy's still labeled "Frank Amy". But she was so drunk at that point she could barely stand up, and in fact a moment later when I took her arm to steady her, she got mad, pulled away, and promptly fell over onto someone.

So there's a part of me that will be relieved not to have that to deal with, at the same time I'll feel so very alone. That's always a confusing combination. And I've always struggled with social situations on my own where I default to feeling like an outsider.

But this is where I am now, and I don't want to deprive myself of great experiences because I might feel uncomfortable.

Reflections: The greater context for this post in my life is that I've struggled as long as I can remember with feeling like an outsider even in groups I clearly belong in and am valued in. I can't count the number of times I've been in a social or group situation where I don't know many people, trying to get up the nerve to talk to strangers – which usually means inserting myself into an existing conversation. I've gotten a lot better at it, but the feelings are still alive and well. Amy either didn't have that obstacle or overcame it with alcohol, so going to a large event like AFF was a lot easier with her, and not just because I wasn't alone. She'd sometimes tell me to go socialize instead of hanging around her, and I take that challenge to heart now.

Amy at the Austin Film Festival, 2015

May 27, 4:59 PM

The dark object in the bathtub is a stool wrapped in a garbage bag, which Amy sat on.

Her body only sweated when she was ill, and it didn't produce odor (even her farts didn't stink), so she rarely needed to bathe.[110]

My rule about changes around the house to Amy-related things is that I need to have a reason; I don't want to change things just to change them. Well, I need that stool finally, so I just took the time to grieve before using it.

Given how much she hated her body even when it was unhealthily skinny, I can't imagine how overwhelming her post-sepsis body was to her. Having to wash it while sitting on a stool would've been like a nightmare.

With these sorts of things I have to feel both sides: how hard it was to know how she felt about her body and be unable to help in any direct way, and also how relieved I am that she doesn't have to struggle with it any more.

----

110   April 5, 9:33 PM

Reflections: "I don't want to change things just to change them" – this remains an important rule, because as time goes on, I find myself looking at things of Amy's that I've left in place, and thinking "It's gotta be time to put that away." No, it doesn't have to be time. The mere elapsing of days and months means nothing inherently for my grieving process. On the flip side, as I've become more functional and resumed working toward goals, it's easy to slide into a status quo in which I'm not giving myself much time to grieve. Oh, those balancing acts!

May 29, 11:00 AM

Amy had a Husbands List, which she explained as celebrities she would happily marry if I suddenly dropped dead.

I thought it was just a mental list, but I just found an actual list on her phone. Aside from Sean Penn and Vince Vaughn, I can understand all of these.

Mark Ruffalo
Johnny Depp
Sean Penn
Jon Stewart
John Cusack
Anthony Bourdain
Vince Vaughn
Stephen Colbert
Owen Wilson
Jake Gyllenhaal
Joseph Gordon-Levitt

Reflections: This was not something I felt comfortable with. It wasn't a serious thing — more of a way of characterizing celebrities she was attracted to. Talking about it amused her, which was good, but part of me always thought, "Why are you telling me about other men you want to marry?" Looking at it now, I see both that I felt insecure and that she felt secure enough with me to be so open about these attractions. It cracks me up that she kept an actual list, and I'm glad she talked about it.

May 30, 9:39 AM

Last night as I did my usual pre-bedtime sobbing[111] – still a useful ritual to make sure I put some attention on my grief at least once a day – I was dwelling on the struggle that, on the one hand my life is going in an exciting direction, while on the other hand I'd give it all up to have Amy back.

But I don't actually have that choice. I don't get to have Amy back. I only get to move forward, and the day will even come when I'll have to let go of that "I'd give it all up" idea in order to fully embrace moving forward.

Anyway, last night I was reminded that Amy wants me to be happy, and then an image suddenly popped up, of a cartoony pointing hand sign that said "This way lies happiness". It felt so Amy-like, and I busted out laughing.

And it just hit me that these insights and helpful humorous messages only happen because I make space for the grief.

---

111 March 7, 9:51 PM

Reflections: This was, and is, a major milestone for me, to see the significance of the fact that moving forward is the only thing worth dwelling on. It's not only a waste of time to think things like "I'd give it all up to have Amy back," but doing so keeps me from making the most of the life I have now. It once again boils down to either clinging or letting go – but I had to cry my way to the point that I could usefully see this. I doubt I'd have been able to hear it if someone had said it in the beginning.

May 31, 11:55 AM

It took me two months, but I got Amy's death certificate altered to include factors related to her military service: PTSD and major depressive disorder. She was discharged in 1999 for PTSD and bulimia.

During her 8+ years in the Air Force, she was stationed in Texas, Mississippi, Japan, and California, but she was deployed at various times to the Persian Gulf, the Kosovo War, and an airplane crash in the Philippines. She didn't talk much about how PTSD affected her, but I know whenever we flew, she needed to sit as close to the front of the plane as possible.

Obviously PTSD alone drives many veterans to drink. In Amy's case, it built on the anxiety she'd developed as a child, and the more anxious she felt, the more she drank.

And drinking at all was something she didn't start in earnest until her military service, but by the time she was discharged her letters reflected a lot of heavy drinking.

The sacrifices people make as a result of military service reach far beyond death on active duty.

June 1, 10:31 AM

I'd completely forgotten that our books all have this stamp. I *think* that it's something Amy was already doing with her books, and that when we joined book collections we agreed this would be the mark of our library.

Our library. Filling – and spilling out from – three floor-to-ceiling bookshelves. Representing Amy's love for modern literature and my love for ancient/medieval history and sci fi/fantasy literature, as well as our shared college experiences.

I've already found myself contemplating limited bookshelf space, that there are books of Amy's I'd never read and could pass on to someone else.

But now... our library. Marked with ink on paper, an appropriate symbol of the fact that we predate the digital computer. A remarkable act of faith in me on Amy's part, that after two divorces she could still believe "this one will stick".

So the thought of parting with any of Amy's part of our library now fills me with guilt. A guilt which in this context is just another form of refusing to let go. I don't for a moment believe that she would now think ill of me for giving away some of her books (there are, of course, certain ones I'll always keep).

The magic this owl accomplishes is making each book that bears it a part of Amy in a way that simply having been Amy's apparently doesn't for me. And I still fervently want to cling to every part of her.

Reflections: I think the guilt I referred to is waning. But the urge to cling to every part of Amy thrives yet in me. I can let go of earrings or clothing Amy hardly wore because their Amy Quotient is low – I don't associate them with her. I can, with appropriate sobbing first, let go of some things with a higher Amy Quotient.

June 2, 11:34 AM

I've decided to let Amy's subscription to the[112] *The New Yorker*[113] expire this month. It's a painful choice, but I think it makes sense.

She might've had this subscription for at least 20 years, and it's almost the only literary thing she read these recent years, and it's just such an Amy thing. All the NYC culture reviews – even though she hadn't been back to the city in decades, I know she still loved it – the mix of fiction and non-fiction, the chance of learning about all sorts of subjects, the cartoons...

I enjoy the occasional piece, but most of them I have to force myself to read. I wish, oh how I wish I were as into it as Amy was. I'd love to be that person, but right now I'm not.

And the crux of the struggle is that I feel like I'm disappointing her. Before Amy, I didn't even watch or read the news. She never stopped pushing me to better inform myself about the world, and that's possibly the main reason I've made the effort I have with this magazine.

I do feel like she's told me to stop apologizing,[114] so as painful as this is, I'm choosing to let go of this potentially longstanding part of her. I'll keep the two issues she was reading, and finish the stack shown here. And, of course, cry my heart out, as I'm doing right now.

---

112 It amuses me to use both definite articles.

113 February 16, 9:42 PM / March 14, 11:50 AM / April 17, 9:07 AM

114 March 6, 2:22 PM

Reflections: *Despite all the thoughts and Amy-voice moments and re-evaluations I'd shared before this, the fear of disappointing Amy had been a hard one to shake. The need to keep up habits and traditions of hers drove me in the first couple months. It's weakened over time, but still kicks in around special events, holidays, and so on. She wanted more consistency from me than my oft-addled brain could provide, so I did serially disappoint her, and maybe this comes out of that. Interestingly, since I made this decision, I've only read a couple of the issues in that stack. I tell myself that's because I'm prioritizing this book, so the proof of the pudding will come once I finish.*

June 3, 11:58 AM

As I've grieved over various aspects of losing Amy, I've realized that many of them really boil down to "I miss you". So rather than getting caught up in or confused by, for instance, what-ifs or whys, I try to go straight to that heart of it.

But some things don't simplify that way, and one of them is that I had to watch her die.[115] That experience itself was traumatic, above and beyond what it represents.

I arrived at the hospital that Wednesday having no idea how much time she had, but hoping, of course, that it was more like half a day or a day – she'd been stable for three days, after all.

So the shock started the moment I walked into her room to see her gasping for breath. As I reached the bed, I saw that her eyelids were partially open but her pupils were hidden – she couldn't see. When I sat on the bed next to her and took her hand and told her, "I'm here, my love," and squeezed her hand, I got no response.

There were a couple times she tried to say something, but it came out unintelligible. I'd like to believe, of course, that she was trying to tell me she loved me. But my experience was that we didn't get to say goodbye.

I am grateful that St. Vincent's allowed me there at all as a visitor, considering many hospitals were forbidding all visitors [because of Covid]. And the idea of missing the final hour of her life is a horrible one – one I know countless people have had to endure during the pandemic.

But I'm nowhere near the point that the gratitude outweighs the grief. The whys come fast and heavy.... why couldn't the doctor've told me sooner that she was dying? Why did she have to go so quickly? Why couldn't I have gotten there in time to even look in her eyes or feel her squeeze my hand? The difference between getting an interactive moment like that

---

115   February 20, 7:42 AM

and what actually happened feels like as much a chasm as the difference between what happened and not being allowed in the hospital.

I'm sure that in time the gratitude will prevail, as I get the pain out. For now, though, it's still agony all the way.

Reflections: The speed with which she died is the one element I'm still having the hardest time with. I can't believe it happened that way, and it feels unfair. To expand on something I alluded to earlier,[116] I had hardly any time to grieve the possibility that Amy might die, before she actually did. We'd been told on Monday that she was eligible for a liver transplant if it came to that. It wasn't till Tuesday night I found out that was incorrect; she wasn't eligible because she hadn't been sober for six months. That was maybe an hour before I went to bed. I needed a week just to grieve that, but I'd only been up a couple hours the next morning when I got the call that "she's dying on us." And naturally, grief for her death has preoccupied me. It's tricky to go back and focus on that brief period when I suddenly knew I might lose her.

116 April 14, 11:49 AM

June 4, 11:05 AM

Life is complex, and the interplay between the different forces and factors that shape us – as well as the choices we make – is also complex.

I don't have a good sense of who Amy was as, say, a toddler. I do know that by high school she'd concluded that pretending to be happy, even when she wasn't, would get her more of the attention she craved.

Just about anyone who met her can speak to how charming she could be. It was a long-practiced mode she could go into in a heartbeat, no matter how she was feeling.[117] On the one hand, that disconnect set her up to struggle with feelings like, "No one understands me and I feel alone", "People only like me for what I do for them", and "I have no inherent worth". As she endured violence and war and divorce and medical sagas, the gap between being charming and how she felt inside must've grown into a gulf.[118]

On the other hand, it's clear from what people said in her memorial that she made a difference in their lives. And I can't believe it was all fakery on her part. For the past twenty years, at least – since she became a Quaker – I know she made a conscious effort to stay positive as part of her desire to contribute to a more peaceful world.

That choice Amy made early on, to pretend to be something she didn't necessarily feel like inside, got her through her life. It undoubtedly contributed to her success in the Air Force. It drew men to her, which gave her Brooklyn (okay, now I'm crying). And so on.

Despite the emotional struggles it created for her, I don't think it was inherently a bad thing. It gave her a way of being in the world that helped her make the world more the way she wanted it to be.

I think that in a sense, she redeemed this early choice – she found a way to take something that could've been only a source of pain for her, and get something good out of it. I find that an encouraging thought.

---

117   March 15, 11:17 AM

118   February 12, 10:56 AM

Reflections: An additional complexity is that Amy could use her charming mask to cover for or attempt to ameliorate the self-destructive and negative behavior she was capable of as an addict. But the main point here is that as she struggled to deal with, on the one hand, wanting the attention she got when she put on her Mask of Charming, but on the other hand, then feeling alone and used, she still managed to make peoples' lives better. I find it encouraging to think that good can come out of our behavior even when our motives are a mixed bag.

June 6, 9:26 AM

One of the thoughts that often comes up while I'm grieving Amy is, "How am I supposed to do this without you?"

To a certain extent, it applies to practicalities of daily life, like managing the dynamics of a small pack of corgis. But due to Amy's medical saga, I already knew what it was like to manage most of that by myself.

Primarily, it applies to making my way in life. A life I had constructed with her, and planned to keep building with her for decades more. I had not only signed up for a life with her, but accepted that what she wanted would often come first. I'm supposed to be "doing this" with her.

How do I, for instance, balance honoring what she would've wanted without slavishly adhering to concerns she no longer has? To be so suddenly having only myself to think about, and getting to think only about myself, feels uncomfortable.

I feel like there's more to this question, but I can't seem to put my finger on that right now...

Reflections: Another part of it certainly has to do with the fact that, of course, we knew different things and so could handle more situations together. The example I used of managing daily life, the corgis, is actually a bad one, because while there are some things I did with them by myself, like feeding them, a lot of what we did with them, we did together. But I do think I nailed it with "a life I had constructed with her." In my reflections for May 16, 12:50 PM, I used the phrase "a life built for two," and that has really resonated.

June 8, 10:47 AM

I took the girls [Brooklyn and her girlfriend Ali[119]] to Seaside yesterday, something Amy and I would likely have done at some point this summer. As we wandered into various shops, I found my eyes drawn to the earring displays – and then tearing up.

I've posted before about the history of earrings being my favorite gift to Amy,[120] and apparently that meant more to me than I realized. Several times I found myself looking through the selections to see if she'd like any of them.

I really, really, wanted to get her something. I didn't, since she's not here to wear them. But when I got home, I cried hard at how much I wanted to. It meant so much to me to see the look on her face when she opened a little package and found earrings she liked – and then to see her wearing them. She died wearing a pair I got her.

So here in these photos are two pair I got her for Christmas, that she never got to wear. The pair on the left are from Mystic Nomad in Goldendale,

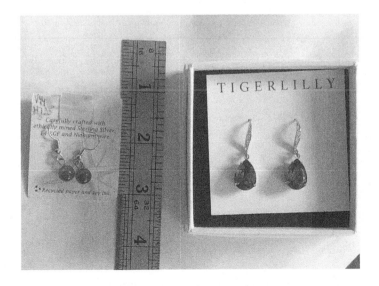

WA, her favorite source. On the right are emeralds, which I chose as [it was] her birthstone.

I'm ready to part with them – anyone want them?

Reflections: I might have given these away too soon – the box on the right is still sitting on the bathroom sink where Amy left it, even though it's empty. So clearly I'm more attached to that pair than I thought, and have more grieving to do.

June 9, 11:00 AM

Today's rumination brought to you by "emmeh, emmeh".

That's my best stab at capturing a noise Amy made sometimes – her most characteristic noise. I guess it's her version of a kind of hopeful grunt. She usually made it in conjunction with an outstretched grabbing motion, and together they meant she wanted a bite of what I was eating.

I loved it. I loved her for it. It was so Amy. Sometimes I'd make the noise if I wanted a bit of what she had, and that always amused her. It's the kind of thing I miss most. So, of course, I'm typing this through tears.

In an ideal world, she might not've needed a noise to communicate that, because she'd have been eating her own food. But after the sepsis, she could rarely eat a full meal, and after her stomach reconstruction surgery, her version of a full meal was a fraction of what it had been. And this past year she was having other eating-related problems to boot.

So most of the time, when I was eating, she wasn't. I'm not sure what I'll do with this noise – I feel like it deserves to be more than just a memory. The simplest solution is obviously to use it myself, and I may get there some day... some day when it doesn't still make me cry.

June 10, 10:57 AM

As I've posted before, I forgave Amy as she died,[121] and I know she forgives me.[122] Forgiving myself is proving more elusive.

That's not because I'm hard on myself, but because every day I wanted to do better by her – to let go of resentment, to listen better, to remember more, to go out of my way to make her feel special, and so on.

I can see that knowing I accomplished the one thing I most fundamentally, most fervently wanted – to somehow show her unconditional love in a way she could see – should be enough. But I'm not there yet.

Then there's something else I've posted about, that for much of our daily life, Amy appeared to be unhappy with me, not trying to pretend to be okay, and taking some of her pain out on me.[123] Early in life I developed a desperation to make girls/women I love happy, and that made this behavior of Amy's particularly painful.

As you can see, I have plenty of reasons to forgive myself, but I think the best path forward is to realize that there is, in fact, nothing to forgive myself for – that the feeling there IS, is mistaken.

I think if Amy were here, she'd put her arms around me and say, "You did it just right."

---

121 March 3, 9:07 PM

122 February 25, 10:20 PM

123 February 12, 10:56 AM

Reflections: When I said "that the feeling there IS, is mistaken," I was referring to my February 5, 8:54 AM post, in which I talked about the fact that while a feeling is valid, it may or may not be literally true. So in this case, while it makes sense that I'd feel like there are things from my relationship with Amy I need to forgive myself for, that's not actually true. It's hard to separate those, which is why the thought that I did it just right is so helpful.

June 11, 10:18 AM

It's easy to think, "why is this only now sinking in?" I have some experience with choosing my perspective: when I find myself unhappy in a situation, I try to ask myself two questions, "can I do anything to change this?" and "if so, am I willing to do something to change it?" If the answer to either one is "No", then I might as well let go of the unhappiness. Of course, that's not so easy, but it's a great starting place.

In a similar vein, it struck me that while it's easy to think that if I'd just gotten to have a mutual moment with Amy at the end, like I posted about recently[124] – to look in each others' eyes, to squeeze each others' hands – then I'd be content, the truth is probably that I'd always want to have had more. More interaction, more time, more... Amy.

So the choice itself seems straightforward. I can stay focused on what I didn't get, on what I wish had happened – or I can focus on what I did get, which is being in the hospital, with Amy, at the end. And the first option really only gets me unhappiness!

As I said, letting go of the unhappiness-begetting choice is the hard part, but the clarity of knowing what I want to reach for sure does help. Now I just need to *remember* that I figured this out…

---

124 June 3, 11:58 AM

Reflections: This is such a helpful way to look at it, because the way it all went down the week Amy died was still torturing me. This perspective got me a lot closer to the balance I referred to in my June 3, 11:58 AM post, in which my gratitude for getting to be there at the end outweighs the grief.

June 13, 9:37 AM

It's been five months. Almost half a year. There's so much I could say, to mark this day...

It still hurts like hell that Amy's gone. It can still take my breath away. What really strikes me, though – and what I haven't written about yet – is how fast time feels like it's passing. Half a year is a meaningful fraction of how long I was with Amy, and it's gone by in a flash.

This feeling isn't new. I first noticed the sense of time speeding up when I started college, and it kept going for decades.

Until Amy. Something about life with her slowed down my experience of time. Instead of "where did the last year go?" it became "last year seems like so long ago." And that meant a great deal to me – time passing quickly is terrifying!

I might guess it was being home (either unemployed or working remotely) so much that made the difference, except that I've been home since January too. It can't be having delightful corgis to surprise and entertain me all day long, because they're still here.

I fear it was Amy herself who made the difference, and the idea of the rest of my life speeding by this fast is a horrible one. I desperately hope I figure out it was something else that I can reproduce.

My best guess is that it was how full and varied our life together was, that kept each week from being a repeat of the previous one. And it's certainly true that much of this year so far has been kept artificially homogeneous by the ever-present pain of losing Amy. So I have some reason to believe it'll get better.

Reflections: A science-minded friend commented that science reporting seems to agree: "You can slow your perception of time by doing new things and experiencing ongoing novelty (like children have without having to work for it)." That was my guess, and it speaks to something fundamental in my relationship with Amy that I was having such an experience with her. She kept life fresh. And it's also true that having grief ever-present on the surface would have made those first five months feel much the same every day. Lately time has felt like it's passing more slowly, which is an enormous relief, and does match up with when I started doing new things again.

June 14, 9:20 AM

At some point in the last year or two, Amy and I watched a British competition show (whose name eludes me[125]) about people constructing float-type scenes and objects out of plants.

One of the competitors had a basket he called a trug, and Amy loved it – she said she wanted one. So I put it on my list of gifts, and was planning to get her one this year for her birthday.

I don't know what she'd have done with it, since she stopped gardening with me several years ago, and I'm not even sure she went out to look at the garden last year. But it wouldn't have been the first gift I got her that I wound up using more.

125 The name of the show was *The Big Flower Fight*.

It's unlikely I'd have gotten one for myself, since my existing gardening kit seems adequate. Well, this one found me. It formed the heart of the flower display Amy's family got for her funeral in February, which I took home with me. So when all the flowers had wilted and I removed everything else making up the display, this perfectly usable basket was left.

A classic trug seems to be wooden with a rounded bottom, rather than wicker with a flat bottom like this one. So maybe this is just a basket. But I'm going to call it a trug, and use it like one anyway – just as I would've with Amy.

Reflections: On a practical level, the difference between what gardening was like for me that spring and what it was like the previous year is minimal, since Amy didn't participate either time. But because we had done yardwork and gardening together in the early years, and because the hope was always that she'd get stronger and join me again some day, the first couple months of gardening this year were painful. I felt her absence keenly. The whole yard felt different – it even felt like it meant something different, since Amy's tastes and sensibilities were what drove much of the yardwork I did.

June 15, 9:33 AM

Behold the first major change I've made around here since Amy died.

When we moved in, we had a papasan chair that Amy, B, and the dogs all shared. Since even at that time, Amy was the primary TV watcher (mostly due to insomnia), that chair got the prime spot in front of the TV, and the couch was along the left wall – facing the bookshelf rather than the TV.

Then the recliner replaced the papasan chair, leaving the overall arrangement the same. So for the past six years I've been watching TV without being able to face the TV, having to look right or sit sideways, etc.

It occurred to me about a month ago that I could actually change that now... This room is no longer Amy's bedroom. It doesn't need to serve her needs. I can make it work for me.

This arrangement lets everyone look straight ahead at the TV, makes it much easier to use the pull-out sofa bed, and makes the room feel bigger.

The things Amy had on the stool by the recliner are still there, as are most of the things she had on the bookshelf – there's only so much change I can make at one time! But while, of course, I'm having a good cry over this, it'll make my life better and improve the experience of guests.

And I know Amy would approve.

Reflections: I still sometimes cry at the layout of the room, or what it means, anyway. So much of our time together was watching TV and movies with her in the recliner next to the bookshelf. Now my memories don't match the room, which jabs a finger in the wound. I'm not second-guessing my reorganization — just continuing to grieve.

June 15, 10:57 AM

I was just checking Amy's email, and had to stop to sob when I saw that Michael Franti and Spearhead are playing at the Edgefield this fall.

We saw them at Maryhill[126] a couple years ago. A beautiful day, good music, lots of love and dancing – it should be a lovely memory.

But she got so drunk she couldn't stand up at the end. So drunk a concerned woman evaluated her for a stroke. It was awful. I have way too many mixed memories like this, and I sure do hope some day I can let go of the bad parts to enjoy the good parts fully.

---

126 The Maryhill Winery in Goldendale, WA, has a large amphitheater that serves as a music venue.

Reflections: This was one of two times that fall Amy got so drunk she couldn't stand. I'm pretty sure it prompted one of the rare occasions on which I said something to her about her drinking – always focused on how scared I was, so she'd be less likely to feel defensive. She did cut down some, and never got that drunk again, which is an example of why I felt so hopeful when I took her to the hospital this last time, that she'd be able to quit: I knew she was capable of controlling her alcohol intake. Back to the topic of forgiving myself, it's really hard not to wish I'd spoken up more often about her drinking, since it seemed to get through to her. But I was terrified of pissing her off and leading her to feel even more isolated in her drinking – a real danger for alcoholics.

June 16, 8:41 AM

Myra turns eight today. And boy has that number set me off – Myra's only a little younger than the time I had with Amy. Plus, Myra's kind of like Amy in dog form; it may not be a coincidence that "Myra" contains "Amy".

Somehow Amy's favorite nickname for Myra got lost in my brain for a couple months. I think it was March before I remembered that Amy called her "Mighty" a lot, in honor of her indomitable watchdogness.

Well, I only just remembered another Myra-related Amy word: Splootsa-My. "My" is short for "Myra", and you can look up what "sploot" means if you need to.[127] Splootsa-My is what Amy called her when she was splooting – which she does much more than the boys do.

I miss the woman whose mind would come up with "Splootsa-My". That verbal playfulness more than anything else is what I fell for when we first met 32 years ago. To have it in my life and then lose it is just excruciating.

---

127 "Sploot" describes a way some dogs lie down: on their bellies, in a straight line, with their hind legs sticking out behind them — the same basic arrangement as when standing up. It can be a verb and a noun.

Reflections: My memory has been affected by grief to a degree I find profound. Even after I posted this, it would be another week or two before I recovered the matching term Sweetsa-My, which Amy used when Myra would come looking for affection. It took me three months or so to remember her favorite nickname for Merlin: "Monkey," which characterized how wild he was as a puppy. How could I forget any of these things?

June 17, 9:05 AM

I was watching the credits of a movie the other night, noticing lots of Italian names, and for some reason that reminded me of telling Amy of all the Armenian and Italian classmates I had in high school (hi folks!), culminating with our discovery that Linda had been her dorm mate at Bard.

And because Grief, that got me thinking of how much I'd shared with her about my life – and how much there is to share with someone at my age.

And it hit me like a wall how much I don't want to have to do that again. I'd been in a relationship before for twenty years without marrying, but after six months with Amy, I wanted to marry her.

I chose her. She was the one I wanted for the rest of my life. That was supposed to be it.

My heart is open, and large enough to contain multitudes (including all of you, with lots of room for more) so emotionally the idea of loving again is easy. But for some reason right now the getting-to-know-each-other part feels like too much.

Reflections: And the fact is, of the five relationships I've had, four of them developed with people I already knew. I don't know how people do the serial dating thing, having to tell person after person after person about themselves. So it's not actually a surprise that I'd find myself feeling the way I describe here. It is, however, absolutely true that the idea of loving again feels easy. I've always tended in that direction, and the healing I've done through grieving seems to have opened me up even more.

June 18, 8:46 AM

Here's the first short film Amy and I made, *Mayhem in Mosier*. Amy knew that in addition to my passion for screenwriting, I'd loved being a PA[128] on a couple short films for friends of mine, so in 2014, about a month before a local 72-hour film project, she proposed we take a shot at it.

https://vimeo.com/105077649

Like I was going to say no to that! While there was a theme and a sound effect each team would get to start the 72-hour period, the rules didn't say you couldn't write a script ahead of time, so we did that. That meant we still had to shoot and edit the thing in 72 hours.

We decided to do a silent black & white comedy piece, flipping the genders of the "villain ties damsel to the railroad tracks" trope. And Amy came up with the brilliant idea of using hashtags and lolspeak for the dialogue

---

128 Production assistant

cards.

We enlisted Ayesha to join us as the actors, and Emily for costuming. I put together a shot list, and we did it with our iPhones over Friday/Saturday. Editing it all together with music and everything in 24 hours was crazy, but we'd have done it except that a random tree branch took out our power. So I carried our desktop computer over to her ex's place, but we still didn't quite make the deadline. The contest was kind enough to accept our submission to show outside of competition.

For some reason we couldn't make it the next weekend when all the submissions were shown, but we heard that ours was an audience favorite.

I still love this film. Every time someone came to visit, I'd make them watch it, and Amy grew more embarrassed by it as time went on. I don't know why! I might actually find it funnier now than I did back then.

Reflections: I can't emphasize enough – it means the world to me that Amy wanted to do this with me. It was easily the furthest she went into the industry I want to work in. Since she'd always been a creative person, it's not a total surprise she'd enjoy it. Her growing embarrassment at the comedy of this short film spurred her to do something serious, which led to our second short – and that one won an award for best adaptation, which she as the director got to accept. Our collaboration was hardly smooth. We argued a lot while preparing to make these movies, and argued a lot about the credits, and argued a lot when film festivals kept listing me as the director because I was the submitter. Yet she kept wanting to do it with me, and I think we were figuring out how to handle it all better. So I was already sad about our languishing third movie, which we'd started writing before the sepsis. For years she kept the script nearby, and kept assuring me she'd get to it. At some point she put it out of sight and out of reach. I don't think she'd given up entirely, but her health was just not going in the right direction these past couple years. As emotional as the idea is, I'm dedicated to making the movie in her honor.

June 20, 10:41 AM

Before I reconnected with Amy in 2012, the trajectory my life was on didn't include fatherhood in any form, and I was okay with that. I got along well with pre-teens, and could see that I made a difference for the ones I got close to.

I've posted before about how unexpected my bond with Brooklyn was,[129] but here's more detail. I walked into Amy's apartment, and B was sitting on the couch, playing a game on her Kindle. I made no assumptions about how she would or should react to me. I sat down next to her, and she just started telling me about the game (I *think* it was Plants. vs. Zombies).

That door she opened on first contact stayed open, and after I moved out to live with them, I quickly became B's favorite adult. That spring, when we learned Amy was pregnant, B was the one who suggested that since her initials are BOW, the new kid's initials could be WOW. So that was what led to choosing Wolf Owen Worsley (I still have the list of W and O names we considered).

The prospect of becoming a biological father, of seeing my new human grow up from scratch, was so... I don't even know what the words are. I started talking to him through Amy's belly, wanting to make a connection as soon as possible.

At some point in there we got results from a genetic screening, and Wolf had indicators for Down's Syndrome or something like that. As I recall, Amy wasn't sure she wanted to go through raising a child with that kind of challenge. She'd also miscarried twice before, so she was watching her pregnancy like a hawk, and after twelve weeks, the signs started.

I'll never forget the moment the radiologist concluded she couldn't find a heartbeat.

I don't have to tell you how devastating that is. The complicating factor is, I think it's quite possible that raising Wolf might have destroyed our marriage. This was so early on for us, before Amy had seen me stand with

---

129 May 10, 4:04 PM

and by her in need, before she felt safe with me. She had firm opinions about parenting that I disagreed with. With Brooklyn, I just went along with her approach for the most part.

But for my own child, I'd have needed to do it more my way, which was incompatible with hers. So what do I do with all this? Losing Wolf is still agony, but losing Amy from trying to parent him with her would have been at least as bad. Life can be so complex... and now I just have to grieve both of them.[130]

---

130 March 15, 2:19 PM

Reflections: I think of Wolf as "the boy who never got to be." To have to grieve the loss of a child without the one I made him with, the only other person who felt the same pain I do — that feels like a particular kind of cruelty.

June 21, 9:21 AM

The phenomenon of "courting behavior" – in which someone behaves one way while developing a romantic relationship, then behaves another way once they're married or have otherwise "secured" the relationship – has been familiar to me for a long time.

I'll never know for sure what motivated it, but that captures what I experienced with Amy.

For the first four months at least, she was universally positive about me and seemed to either agree with or support most of what I believed. I know Amy well enough to believe that everything she said in the beginning, she believed in the moment. And I've posted before about other aspects of that period, like how she often brought me lunch when I was working from home – with loving messages written on the napkins.[131]

When we first reconnected that previous summer, it felt to me like an enormous weight was holding her down. I think that was a low point in her life, having seen her second marriage fall apart, being unemployed and too sick to work, and still unable to shake her eating disorder despite program after program (including three months at Johns Hopkins).

My sense is that my re-entry into her life was a ray of light she never thought she'd see again, and she just felt overwhelmingly grateful for me, my gentleness, and my acceptance.

But by the time we married in late March, her behavior and attitude toward me had changed dramatically. She was often judgemental, resorting to shame, blame, criticism, and ridicule. The glowing opinions she'd expressed before never really resurfaced to that degree.

That contrast in behavior really hurt, and remained painful for the rest of our time together. One of the things that has always mattered most to me is what someone I love thinks of me. Amy's positive regard for me in the beginning is undoubtedly the lion's share of why I left Portland to be with her as fast as I did.

---

131 May 19, 8:58 AM

It helped when I realized that, as I've posted about before,[132] I'd managed to give her a safe enough space that for the first time she didn't have to hold it together, and could show her struggle. Helped, but didn't outweigh the pain.

I still feel that pain, but now it's just one more thing to grieve. A couple years ago (I may have mentioned this before[133]) when she opened her Valentine's Day card and gift, she said "Every day is Valentine's Day with you," and knowing what I know now, and having forgiven her, I think that underneath all her pain and fear and anger, that was indeed true.

---

132   February 12, 10:56 AM

133   February 14, 11:06 AM

Reflections: Posts like this might make it seem as though I'm having epiphanies that suddenly make a big difference, but these realizations don't usually change how I feel in a dramatic immediate way — they don't wipe away the pain, and as we've seen, sometimes I forget them entirely! It's incremental progress, and each one bolsters the benefit of the others.

June 23, 11:05 AM

I just spontaneously recovered another sweet thing I'd call Amy. I've mentioned before that I often called her "my Amy"[134] – well, I'd also call her "mon Ami" as a pun, since she was my friend, the French word for which sounds like her name.

Considering how crappy my memory recall continues to be, these random recoveries give me hope.

---

134 January 24, 11:54 AM

June 23, 3:42 PM

Today's random emotional heartbreaker is getting in line at the grocery store, then spotting these.

Amy loved sour candy, the more sour and less sweet the better. She wanted it to make her scrunch up her face.

And for some reason, during her three-month hospital stay for sepsis, she particularly wanted it. I soon discovered which market in the area had the ones she liked most.

Trying not to cry into my mask[135]…

---

135   My Covid pandemic face mask

Reflections: *The double punch (unintended pun alert) of sour gummies is that they don't just remind me of Amy, but remind me of her in her direst time. Her three-month sepsis recovery in the hospital was a saga that revolved around her guts. She'd almost died, and had been cut open both to relieve the pressure from the infection and to try to find the source, so vomiting was particularly painful and dangerous for her, but being hospitalized always made her more likely to throw up. As a result, her diet was restrictive, and these gummy candies were a harmless treat — but I had to scour all nearby stores for the ones she liked. She only occasionally wanted them at home, so I still mostly associate them with her sepsis recovery.*

June 24, 9:00 AM

Aside from posting here, I've felt... frozen, or something, elsewhere on social media.

It hasn't seemed right to resume posting there without acknowledging Amy's death, and I haven't had the attention to figure that out until now. So I just posted this in her Instagram account, and I'll post something similar in mine. My Twitter account I can probably also adapt this to.

I'm less sure what to do with her Twitter account, since she was really only active around 2016 and had few followers. I might just leave it alone for now.

I still hate having to do all this. But it's part of letting go, I think, which is the opposite of denial. And denial just keeps part of me locked up, unable to live. And living is probably the single best way to honor Amy.

Reflections: Her Instagram account name was Myra_and_Meatloaf_and_Merlin, and she posted mostly about our corgis.[136]

136 *January 18, 3:47 PM*

This account was run by Amy Heil, who passed away in early 2021. Corgis had been her dream dog since childhood, so to end up with three of them really was a dream come true for her. She had a full life, including eight years as a nurse in the Air Force, helping build a successful restaurant business, raising a daughter, and three marriages. She was a writer, a cook, a maker, an activist, a filmmaker, a dog foster parent, and much more. Read her obituary at https://www.columbiagorgenews. com/obituaries/obituary-amy-heil/article_8c581fca-7de9-11eb-8963- 37227afa85c2.html.

June 25, 9:00 AM

It's official – yesterday came and no *The New Yorker*[137] arrived in the mail.

I actually emailed them to find out when she first subscribed, and it was January 1999, at the beginning of her last year in the Air Force. So, about 22.5 years.

Why did I want to know that? I had a feeling it was about that long, and it's much harder to let go of something that not only was a meaningful part of Amy's life, but had been so for decades. The more integral something feels to her life, the more I want to cling to it.

Which brings me to my latest realization... I've posted before about the fact that many of the different painful thoughts, whys, what ifs, etc., boil down to "I miss you", and now I see that even that is really just "how do I let you go?"

It may seem, from what I post here, that I'm doing well on the letting-go front – and maybe I am. But it doesn't feel that way.

I left Portland, my home of twenty years, a mere six weeks after Amy and I got together, because I was desperate to be with her. Prior to that, every time I had to drive back after being with her all weekend, I'd bawl my way home. And desperation played a huge role in why I lived in the hospital with her for the first month of her sepsis ordeal, and why I stayed nearby for her remaining two months in the hospital.

Letting go hits right up against all that desperation. I don't think there's a deeper level to my grief than that.

---

137 June 2, 11:34 AM

THE
NEW YORKER

Your Subscription Has Expired

Account Number: ▓▓▓▓▓▓▓▓

Expiration Date: June 2021

Renewal Rate: $149.99

REACTIVATE

Reflections: This is one of the few examples of a realization that did significantly change my grief experience in the moment. "How do I let you go?" has become the center of my grieving – more on that in posts yet to come. And the truth is that even before Amy and I got together, I had held onto her in my heart for more than twenty years. So I have an enormous amount of emotional momentum in clinging to Amy.

June 28, 8:34 AM

I've begun working in earnest on the book.[138] This week's focus is turning the messy copy/paste results from Facebook into actual text in chronological order.

Then July's focus is adding notes containing emotional context to some posts, stuff that I didn't or couldn't fit into the original Facebook post but that I think might be meaningful to the reader. I really do want that to be emotionally-oriented material rather than informationally-oriented.

So hopefully by August I'll have turned it all over to my editing and design team (go Honor and Leslie!).

At one point in late 2015 when Amy was in the ICU with sepsis, early on when it wasn't clear if she'd make it, I remember being sustained by the sense that she still had work left to do in the world.

I feel like this book is part of that work, even if she's no longer in the world, and I love being a team with her across the life-death divide.

---

138   April 23, 8:43 AM

Reflections: You may have noticed that whereas earlier I usually posted more frequently, at this point the posts come once a day for the most part. I was posting more about other things, and didn't necessarily find myself with anything Amy-related to say, which both seem like healthy developments. Sometimes when I'm doing my nightly Ritual of the Shirt, as I'm crying, I'll say things like, "We're going to help some people!" And I started crying after typing that, so meaningful is it.

June 29, 11:12 AM

I posted on February 2nd about putting away the last clothes Amy wore,[139] and that was true. But they weren't the last clothes of hers that need putting away.

These are clean clothes – underwear and socks in the basket, and shirts hung up to dry in the bathroom, all where she put them. I think it was late February before I even noticed those clothes were still there (even under normal conditions, I have a well-developed ability not to notice things around me).

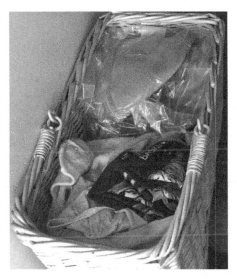

And having felt like I'd passed the milestone of dealing with Amy's clothes, only to discover I hadn't, seems to have made it much harder to reach. I think about putting these away, and I might sometime soon. I also might not – there's no hurry.

The main purpose of the basket was originally to hold stuff that needs to go upstairs (because Amy, in her mild OCDness, couldn't tolerate stuff just

---

139 February 2, 12:34 PM

sitting on the stairs), but as she lived more and more downstairs, and went upstairs less, she started using it as a storage place for clothes she was going to use soon.

Reflections: *I've put away the shirts for the convenience of the rare guest I have, after a good cry about doing it. But the stuff in the basket is still there. I haven't used that basket at all, in fact, and it could easily be next year before I decide to clean it out. It's another example of not wanting to change something just to change it.*

June 30, 10:19 AM

Last night I discovered that Apple TV has all four seasons of *Fraggle Rock*. While this is clearly a thing of joy, my first reaction was bawling because I can't watch it with Amy.

Actually, my first reaction was "I want to watch it with you!" But in keeping with my recent post about how I think letting go is the fundamental level of my grieving process, I realized that looking at the situation I was facing through the lens of what I want is a kind of clinging.

Saying "I don't get to watch it with you" hurts more because it forces me to face the absoluteness of the loss. There is no hope that I'll ever get to watch *Fraggle Rock* with Amy (given that I really don't believe we do the same things in the afterlife that we did in life).

It sounds so stark and bleak when put that way, but so is the loss I have to face. And of course, it's not really about this TV show – that just stands in for Amy herself. If I don't face Amy's absence in all its fullness, it'll stay with me on some level, rattling around and holding me back from the joy I want, and that I know Amy wants for me.

July 1, 10:17 AM

The latest installment of "John vs. First Person Personal Pronouns"...[140]

I got the mortgage switched over— no, that's the easy way out. I had Amy's name removed from the mortgage. And that was the easy choice too. See, I just had to choose what to put before "mortgage". Logically, I couldn't say "removed from my mortgage" because if it were just mine, there'd be no one else to remove.

I could've used "our mortgage"... but I chose to avoid that. For every choice I post about here in which I take the brave path, there are plenty in which I take the easy way out. The fact that Amy will stay on the house's title until I sell it gives me carte blanche to use "our house", and I have no doubt I'll avail myself of that.

I am, however, trying out "I/me/my" instead of "we/us/our" more often – even if sometimes only in my head.

---

140 January 21, 10:30 PM / April 22, 3:46 PM / May 2, 8:55 AM

July 2, 10:46 AM

Alanis Morissette has a song, "Not the Doctor", that starts like this:

> I don't want to be the filler if the void is solely yours
> I don't want to be your glass of single malt whiskey
> Hidden in the bottom drawer
> I don't want to be a bandage if the wound is not mine

For people who are codependent, chronic caretakers, have trouble setting boundaries, and so on, it's a wonderful anthem. And in my historical context, as I wrote about in the post below,[141] that's what it was for me.

But it hits me differently now. I find myself crying because – to borrow another line from the song – I got to be the glue that held Amy's pieces together. It turned out that enough of me was healthy enough to give her what she needed. Coming from a place of emotional health, I can choose to play a role in someone's life that is healing for them, without martyring myself.

'Choose' is the key word. I have a choice now that I never had before. I don't have to act on an unthinking compulsion. It's a beautiful thing!

---

141 May 6, 3:14 PM. On Facebook, I shared my previous post so if anyone needed to read it again to understand the new post, it was right there for them.

July 4, 10:55 AM

Yes, it's another Alanis Morissette post... long before I had ever considered gratitude as something to practice, her song "Thank U" from *Supposed Former Infatuation Junkie* got to me. Here's the chorus:

Thank you India
Thank you terror
Thank you disillusionment
Thank you frailty
Thank you consequence
Thank you, thank you silence

The particular things she's expressing gratitude for grow out of her trip to India, but somehow this song has made me cry every time I've heard it, even playing overhead in a grocery store. It's a song I have to stop to experience.

Then came Gorge Happiness Month in October 2017, when Emily Reed asked me to keep a journal of what it was like to make a daily practice of acts of kindness, gratitudes, and moments of silence.

It prompted me to create a sort of gratitude prayer that I recite every night. I've posted about it before.[142] I think it was particularly powerful for my relationship with Amy, because even after the worst fights, when I had my darkest thoughts and feelings, I made sure to say the part that's about her.

I knew (as I've also posted about before[143]) that those darkest thoughts and feelings didn't actually represent how I thought and felt about her – they long predated even my meeting her in 1989. I knew they'd pass, even if I had to fight my way out, and my love and regard for her would be there waiting.

Now in addition to being grateful *for* Amy, I'm grateful *to* her, for everything she has given and continues to give me. And most of all, for sharing herself with me as best she could.

---

142 January 24, 11:54 AM

143 February 5, 8:54 AM

Reflections: I can't overstate how vital it was to be able to separate my feelings from reality. There were, to be honest, moments when I felt hate. There were moments when I felt such pain that I thought, *"maybe she'll die."* In those moments, the feelings seemed absolutely real – but some part of me still knew, from my experience with counseling, that they weren't real, that the truth was, I loved Amy and wanted her to live as long as possible. And every time, the moment passed, the horrible feelings crawled back into their hidey holes, and I was able to choose love. When I say I'm grateful for what Amy continues to give me, I'm referring to, for example, the way her values inspire me, or the way she pushed me to better inform myself about what's going on in the world. On some level, in all honesty, those examples constitute clinging to her, to the best parts of her. But that's a level I can work on letting go, while still embracing the inspiration I feel.

July 5, 10:46 AM

When we moved into this house, Amy put a photo of B and this one of me on her side of the bed. I think it was last year I added the photo of her. Mine is my HS graduation portrait, while hers was taken about four years later, so from around the same phase of life in which we first met.

Boy does it feel odd to have a photo of myself on what is now just my bed. And she was never able to sleep in our bed at any point after I put my photo there for her.

It seems like that should make it easy to remove my photo from the headboard, but it's not. Maybe the symbolism would be too close to home – if we as people can't be together in life, at least these photos of us can be together.

As I write this all out through the ever-present tears, it occurs to me... I could put this pair together somewhere else, and replace them with a recent photo of both of us. I like that idea. And now you see how much these posts are me just thinking through things. I start with an idea, but I don't usually know where I'm going from there.

This is just one of so many emotional flies that pester me every day.

Reflections: I have a perhaps overly-developed ability to... from one perspective, it's putting things off, while from another, it's prioritizing. I can see something every day that needs doing, that would take relatively little time, and not do it. I'm not procrastinating, because it's not that I don't want to do it. But it seems less important, day after day, than what I want to get done each of those days. So when I talk about emotional flies pestering me, I mean that moving these photos and replacing them is just one of many examples of Amy-related things around the house that, in this context, I could take a moment to grieve and then change. Right now, though, my priority is this book, so I put off doing these things – which means I suffer the consequence of having the raw nerve of my grief slightly rubbed on all the time.

July 6, 10:42 AM

For the first time in eighteen months, I'm cleaning out the photos on my phone. And it's proving to be a more emotional experience than I anticipated.

It's not just that the photos document my life with Amy – although that would be enough. The unexpected element is that I feel like it doesn't matter what's on my phone any more. I had to stop and think about why that would be. I mean, it's all still my life with Amy even though she's gone.

The thing is, when I imagine *using* the photos and videos on my phone, what comes to mind is being with Amy and us wanting to share a past moment with someone else. And that'll never happen again.

It's curious that being able to share those same moments with someone else but without Amy being there wouldn't feel meaningful to me. Logically I want to be able to do that.

And yet here I am sobbing at how strongly I feel like it just doesn't matter now. All I can think is, this is a feeling I need to acknowledge and let out, but not act on.

Reflections: This is such a curious thing, but it's true: it feels like the whole point of keeping photos and videos on my phone is so that when Amy and I are talking to someone and sharing something about our life – the corgis, or Brooklyn's cosplay, or a Maker Faire[144] – we can pull up a related visual. It took me months to realize that whereas Amy was perfectly comfortable doing that with someone she'd just met, I rarely am. So the feeling is that without her, it's never going to happen, and therefore it doesn't much matter what I keep on my phone.

144   A Maker Faire is a DIY festival celebrating human ingenuity and creativity, from multinational corporations and regular people alike. We regularly attended the flagship event in the Bay Area every year, as well as an annual "mini-Maker Faire" in Portland.

July 7, 11:07 AM

I'm STILL finding stashes of Amy's past. She went to this place in March 2012, about three months before we reconnected, and I have no memory of her mentioning it.

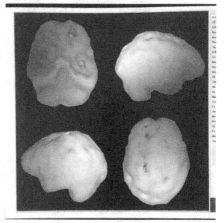

Judging by the summary of her state at the time, she was remarkably honest with them.

In addition to her emotional struggles, she reported dealing with weakness in muscles, rapid/irregular pulse, low blood pressure, nausea/vomiting, chronic abdominal pain, back pain, and more.

Emotionally, this passage stands out: "She notes difficulties with depression, with times of feeling both down and tearful as well as a lack of pleasure or joy in life. She notes times of having thoughts about death, but not necessarily having a desire to end her life."

This elaborates on the feeling of heaviness I got from her the first time I visited her that July. The clinic's motto was "Change your brain, change your life" so it's not surprising they did brain scans. The fact that I have pictures (of a sort) of her brain tickles me no end!

After what might have felt to her like baring her soul, and all the tests, their recommendations seem to have boiled down to, "go take these vitamins and minerals", and while the connections between her vitamin and mineral intake and her physical and emotional health were real – and something she knew a lot about, as a nurse – I imagine she felt let down not to get more substantial help.

In the end, what seems to have made the most difference was me, starting with all that reconnecting with me and getting closer to me meant to her. One recurring theme in our early email correspondence was her surprise at being treated with understanding, acceptance, and forgiveness. In 2014 and 2015 she frequently ran into people who hadn't seen her for several years, and they were uniformly astonished at how much healthier and happier she looked.

You can imagine how much it means to me to have gotten to give that to her.

Reflections: I saw Amy struggle frequently with feeling like medical personnel weren't giving her the help she needed. As a former nurse and EMT – and because she was Amy – she often had strong opinions about what she needed, and it was easy for her to feel like doctors didn't really listen to her. This could make her a hard person to help. On a practical level, with the ongoing double demons of heartburn and nausea plaguing her to some degree almost constantly, supplements weren't as simple a solution as a doctor might think. So all of that is why I feel fairly certain she felt let down by her experience at this clinic. Her mom had gone there the year before, but it just might not have been a good fit for Amy.

July 8, 5:42 PM

It was a beautiful day for a hike with the visiting Rose.

On the rare occasion Amy and I went on outdoor excursions or day trips, she was always the one who packed lunch, so it felt odd doing that myself. I used her backpack, which is a bit of an emotional minefield with its decorations and unexpected contents (like a baggie full of soap and shampoo samples).

After the hike I picked up my car from the detail shop, and had to put all the items that had been in various pockets and nooks back where they belonged. But that proved to be one emotional straw too many, when I found an unopened pack of alcohol wipes.

Amy found them useful, whereas I've never liked having my hands coated with that cleansing liquid. So I don't know what to do with them, and that kind of broke me for a bit. They also remind me of the days when we went places as a family.

Obviously I love B and Ali dearly, yet without Amy it's hard for me to feel like we're a family. I may have to just make a decision on that. Mostly, though, it all just stirred up how much I miss Amy, and in how many ways I miss her.

And that's to be expected as I get back out into the world and life.

Reflections: Counseling is the gift that just keeps on giving. If I didn't know how to interact with my feelings in something resembling a healthy way, these kinds of experiences might well keep me from getting back out there. As it is, I'm able to use them for healing. The "it's hard for me to feel like we're a family" statement had nothing to do with B or Ali; losing Amy didn't alter my love and affection for either of them. We were a family I only had through Amy, and at the time I wrote this, I felt like I'd lost the emotional linchpin that, for me, had defined "the family." So that's an adjustment I had to give myself time to make – we are still a family, and one I'm deeply grateful to have.

July 9, 11:00 AM

I posted back in February about my habit of getting flowers for Amy every week.[145] They weren't generally anything special, just something from the grocery store's floral department.

Although I enjoyed having flowers around too, it was mostly meaningful to me because it was meaningful to her. What illustrates that is the fact that I've continued getting flowers every week, but the truth is, I rarely notice them. I look at the table and the things on it a lot, but somehow never pay attention to the flowers.

---

145   February 14, 11:06 AM

It's nothing personal... I tune out a lot of things in my daily life, which was a source of conflict between me and Amy. It mostly came up in the kitchen, when I'd notice something was different and she'd tell me she did that last week.

It's like I only care about what's immediately important to me. Logically, if I'm mostly oblivious to having flowers in the house, then it doesn't make sense to keep getting them. But that would mean letting go! *starts crying*

I could also choose to try to change, to practice noticing what's around me. That seems like a good idea – though not an excuse to avoid letting go. Then there's the guilt, as though I'd somehow be letting Amy down if I stopped with the flowers.

This'll take some processing.

Reflections: *The next time I went grocery shopping after writing this, I completely forgot even to look at the flowers. That sure was an eye-opener! I realized then that while the dining table was Amy's first place to put flowers, for me they blend in with the clutter, since I use that table more as a To Do staging area. For a while I tried putting flowers in other places, to see if I'd notice and appreciate them there. This is certainly another area where, at the time, I felt like I'd be letting her down if I stopped. But I suspected I might need to let go of them as a regular practice in the way I did for Amy. Now I've reached a point where occasionally I'll think, "I want flowers this week," but otherwise don't have them around.*

July 10, 9:53 AM

This is Amy's desk, which she hadn't used in years. If any part of the house is in danger of becoming a shrine, it would be this.

When we moved in here, I put my desk in what we dubbed the office. The idea was for it to be *our* office, but we got hung up on how to actually share the space – factors like noise. So her desk stayed here, in a corner of the dining room.

Enter, once again, the sepsis saga. She came home from the hospital with a skin graft on her belly because it was still too big to close up. Sitting in the desk chair wasn't feasible, so we got her a laptop to use on the recliner. And she never went back to the desk.

Brooklyn used the computer before she got a laptop, and some after that for things that benefited from the larger screen (like Minecraft). But it's all mostly just sat there, a reminder of when Amy was relatively healthy.

It's not even a minefield – it's a pile of mines, hitting so many emotional pain points from so many areas of our life and my grieving experience.

And that's okay. There's no hurry – I have as much time as I need to work on letting go.

Reflections: I'm not sure what I was getting at with that putative distinction between a minefield and a pile of mines, but it came from poking through all the stuff she left on the desk. You can't see it, but there's a little woven basket behind the screen that contains all sorts of stuff. I looked through it all fairly early on, when I was desperate for every scrap of Amyness. But I've come to realize that her desk is more than I'm ready to handle. Just thinking about it makes me sob.

July 11, 11:57 AM

Where do I start... most of these pots, etc., are Amy's, as in she had them when we reconnected. Plants, inside and outside, mattered to her. She had a collection of houseplants and a collection of gardening equipment.

She used to garden with me, do yardwork with me, and water her houseplants.[146] By this point you can probably guess what I'm about to say – then came the sepsis.

I think she managed to get out some times into the garden and/or yard in maybe 2017 or 2018, but then even that stopped. Over time she also ceded the houseplant watering to me, which was part of a larger trend in which she gradually stopped doing much housework.

As I was crying over how much I miss the Amy who was well enough to do all those things, it hit me: a good portion of the grieving I've been doing is actually grieving I needed to be doing when she was alive but wasn't.

I could've started grieving years ago over losing the Amy who was well enough to sleep in bed with me at least some of the time,[147] or the Amy who was well enough to go to the grocery store with me,[148] or the Amy who could drive herself anywhere, or...

It's a long list.

---

146   June 14, 9:20 AM

147   March 9, 6:50 PM

148   April 17, 4:16 PM

Reflections: This is such a good point. I could write a long chapter of a book just on the history of Amy and me and bed and nighttime. Ironically, back when Amy came to bed intermittently, I did cry some when she didn't. But at some point I just resigned myself to it unhappily, when I could've kept grieving it. Maybe then I'd have been able to help her think about it, about what we could do to get her back in bed even occasionally. So file this under Things to Learn From.

July 12, 10:46 AM

I've been working for months to get all Amy's data off her laptop so I can give it to Brooklyn's girlfriend, and I'm almost done – including her text messages (via the macOS app), saved passwords, and her browser bookmarks.

It only just now occurred to me that I need to stop and grieve letting go of this.

I posted a couple days ago about Amy's switch from a desk computer to using a laptop on her recliner. This laptop became her office, where she did all her political activism. She put many hours into crafting thoughtful, informed messages to various politicians in support of the Friends Committee on National Legislation and Veterans for Peace.

Being a news junkie, she'd often pull it out to check the news *while* we were watching a movie.

So when I think of Amy and all the time she spent in the recliner, the image is as likely to include this device as not. And for that reason part of me would naturally want to cling to it, but I don't need a second, older, laptop, and Ali needs a replacement for her old Chromebook.

It's possible I might've been so focused on meeting that practical need that I forgot to grieve what it means. I'm grateful for the reminder.

July 13, 10:42 AM

Today marks half a year since Amy died. My sleep has been unusually erratic this past week or more, and I suspect – hope – this is why. There's so much I could say...

I'm relieved that the last month has felt longer than previous months, that time might be slowing down for me.[149] Half a year is a measurable percentage of the time Amy and I had together, and the prospect of years flying by at the rate the first five months did is terrifying.

Mostly I want to talk about letting go. Ever since my realization three weeks ago that letting go is the foundational level of my grief,[150] I've been trying to focus on that. And for every moment of grief I encounter, letting go really turns out to be at the center.

When I came home from the hospital after she died, my starting place was desperately wanting to cling to every iota of anything related to her. And I still feel that way about a lot of things.

But I've found there's a sweet spot, a point at which if I let go of something, I can sob and wail over it in a healing way. Before that point, it can feel traumatic to have to let go, whereas I think [if I wait] too much past that point, it gets harder to access the feelings and I miss the chance to do some healing.

Many of the hardest moments I've faced have been ones in which I was forced to let go of something I wasn't ready to, like when Amy's bank closed her account before I got around to doing it. That feels like something's being ripped away from me.

I'm starting to feel like all these individual things I have to let go of, like taking her name off accounts or being unable to remember where we got this mug or clearing off the stool that served as her side table (haven't done that one yet), are all leading to letting go of Amy herself.

I don't have a clear sense of what that means. It seems like the sort of thing

---

149 June 13, 9:37 AM

150 June 25, 9:00 AM

that could be transformational. I do know that the most common phrase to come up now when I find myself crying over something is, "how do I let you go?", so apparently I'm on my way to finding out what it means.

Who knows – maybe I'm a pupal butterfly preparing to emerge from its chrysalis and spread its wings for the first time.

Reflections: My editors and I had agreed that this book would cover the first six months after Amy's death, so I knew this date would be the ending post. I feel self-conscious about having such an appropriate thing to say. It's not like I was sitting around scheming the perfect ending. A couple days beforehand, I'd realized I had something to say about letting go that I hadn't said yet, and clearly that would make a good end post, so I just waited. It felt strange knowing my relationship to these posts would change once they wouldn't be included in the book. This had become a private blog. As post-worthy thoughts occurred to me, I'd slot them into upcoming days, and I was putting more time (and length) into them than I had been a couple months prior. I'd also been trying to think of topics I wanted to make sure I got into the post. After this post, I could tell I'd post less, and I have mixed feelings about that. On the one hand, there's an argument to be made that it's better to post about my grief as things naturally occur to me – rather than "doing it for the book" – but on the other hand, since I only started each post with a thought, and then figured a lot out as I wrote, I probably gained quite a bit that I wouldn't have if I'd just been posting naturally this whole time. As for letting go of Amy herself, I fell for her in 1989, and carried her in my heart the entire time our lives diverged. We may only have been together for eight-and-change years, but I have 31 years of clinging to deal with.

APPENDIX

ARTICLES BY AND ABOUT AMY

Words matter:
Clarity found in Mom's crumpled crossword

Amy K.W. Heil
Hood River News, January 30, 2019

I'll begin with a confession: We finally removed the last of our Christmas decorations just last week. The debris field from dragging out the desiccated tree looked like a crime scene despite our efforts to contain it. (We'll be vacuuming needles out of the carpet until next December, I'm sure.)

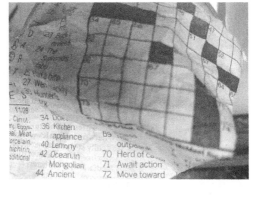

In my defense, as a child we spent Christmas at my Auntie M's every year, and she celebrated the actual Twelve Days of Christmas. That meant decorations remained in her house until the Epiphany: The symbolic representation of when the Christ Child was revealed to the Magi. Religious history lesson aside, it's clear that this year, in our house, the Magi came late. Maybe their GPS took them off course, I don't know, but as I packed the characters from the Creche (Nativity) this morning, I wrapped them carefully in the same newspaper that has cradled them for ages, and wished them a safe journey back to the attic.

The scraps of newspaper that protect our ornaments and decorations are reused every year, until they become too worn or torn to be of use. They envelop an odd assortment of items: Among other things, a rhinestone alligator from a trip to New Orleans, various arts and crafts made by my daughter over the years and, as per German and Family tradition, a whole lot of pickles. (Google it.)

This past year, as I was unwrapping ornaments, my fingers growing filthy from ink, I studied the newspapers, like I always do. I smooth them out into a stack, often checking dates and reading headlines, even perusing a few articles. Just like the sentimental history of the ornaments and decorations they protect, each scrap of paper tells a story.

At one point, I came across a page with a completed New York Times crossword puzzle from September, 2014. It was filled out in ink, without error, in the clear, distinctive handwriting of my mother.

It was a special moment for me, not just because my mother passed away in October of 2017, but for its symbolism as well.

Like every mother/daughter relationship, ours was complicated. We had trouble communicating on many levels, but wherever life took me, I could count on an occasional phone call from her when all we would do is complete the NYT crossword together.

This took place over decades, even when hours, miles, and sometimes continents kept us apart. She could decipher the clues to older references, I the newer stuff, and together we crossed the generational divide — learning about each other and the workings of our minds from what we knew of life, through simple words and phrases. It brought a depth to our relationship that regular attempts at conversation frequently found lacking.

When she was diagnosed with the early stages of dementia, those collaborations changed as her illness rapidly evolved. Over a very short period of time, along with her ability to reason, she started to lose motor functions. Writing became increasingly difficult as her hands began to tremble. She could still fill out the crosswords, but her beautiful script (she studied calligraphy in college) began to degrade as her tremors increased. Before long, writing became indecipherable and then impossible.

Over the same period of time, she rapidly lost her ability to speak and use facial expressions. Dementia is unique to every individual, and for my mother, it was clear that her cognitive functions far outlasted her ability to communicate on most every other level. As the muscles in her face grew still, her eyes grew wider and more eager, and in them I could often see the vestiges of her once brilliant mind.

Having long abandoned our crossword conversations, I was forced to communicate with her using simply my words, and she, the sporadic moments of awareness in her eyes. It might have seemed lopsided, but I knew she was there. It never once crossed my mind, throughout her illness, to speak to her as if she could no longer understand.

I remember sitting next to her once with a crossword puzzle in hand, reading out loud the clues and filling it in the best I could without her input. With her head turned toward me, she struggled to speak in an effort to participate despite her impairment, and I felt that same, unique connection we had shared over the years, simply from playing with words. As I spoke, she listened, and responded by gripping my hand with a strength that eased the trembling, if only for a moment. It was a clear comfort for the both of us, and it left me speechless as well.

I took a picture of that crossword puzzle, then put it back where it belonged in the stack of recycled papers we used to wrap up Christmas this week. At this moment, it could be wrapped around anything from a beady-eyed glittered hedgehog to a fragile glass bell that has been hanging on a Heil Family tree for over 100 years. It only matters that it's there.

I'm comforted by the memories of those moments, sharing words with my mother. I'm also comforted by the thought that those words hold safe, not just sentimental objects, but the memories of her in my heart.

Amy's article can be found online at https://bit.ly/3o5IaOp.

In Memorial: Amy Heil

Columbia Gorge News, March 5, 2021

Amy Katherine Heil was born in Portland, Oregon in 1970, the fifth and youngest child of F. Charles W. Heil and Patricia Willard Heil. She passed away unexpectedly on January 13, 2021 with her husband John at her side.

Known in the family as "Amy Kat," Amy was raised in southwest Portland. She attended West Hills Christian and soon-to-be formerly-known-as Wilson High School, where she sang in the choir and wrote for the school newspaper. She was a bright and creative student who, if all her stories are to be believed, must've had 40-hour days. She studied Political Science at Bard College in New York and at Reed College before joining the US Air Force in 1991. While on active duty she also completed her bachelor's degree at William Carey College.

Amy's eight-year career as a medical technician took her to bases in Texas, Mississippi, Japan, and California. She took every opportunity to excel and exceeded every limit placed before her, and was deployed to the Persian Gulf and to the Balkans. Upon leaving the Air Force she returned to Portland, where she met and married Justin Williams. Their daughter, Brooklyn, is Amy's pride and joy. In 2005 the family moved to Hood River, Oregon, where Amy and Justin opened a successful restaurant, Sushi Okalani; the restaurant's logo is an example of Amy's artistic work.

In 2013 she married John Worsley, and the new family moved to

Mosier later that year so Brooklyn could attend Mosier Community School. Amy supported the charter school enthusiastically, filling their home with art purchased at benefit auctions. She was also the creative force behind two short films she made with John, "Mayhem in Mosier" (2014) and "All Our Sins Remembered" (2016). The latter film won Best Adaptation at the 2016 Columbia Gorge International Film Festival.

As a Quaker, Amy worked passionately for peace, volunteering virtually for the Friends Committee on National Legislation as well as Veterans for Peace, and attending rallies, protests, and marches. She wrote a number of opinion pieces for the Hood River News promoting peace and understanding.

Amy had a playful sense of humor, loved to tell stories, almost invariably charmed those who met her, loved to foster rescue dogs, and was proud of being a "softie" who cried at car commercials.

She will be remembered forever by her husband, John Worsley, of Mosier, Oregon; her daughter, Brooklyn Williams; her daughter-in-spirit, Alison Dye; and by Justin Williams. She is also survived by her father, Chuck Heil (Class of '61), her four siblings and their spouses, her older four siblings (including Benjamin Heil, Class of '84), her nieces and nephew, and her beloved aunt, Margaret Heil. Amy was a devoted pet mom to three Welsh corgis, Myra, Meatloaf, and Merlin.

Donations in Amy's memory may be made to Veterans for Peace (https://veteransforpeace.salsalabs.org/donatevfp/index.html).

Amy's obituary can be found online at https://bit.ly/3i5n5PJ.

Why we do this:
'A dose of peace and Corgi love'

By Amy K. W. Heil
Hood River News, June 10, 2017

This past weekend was a weekend of moments — rife with equal parts tears and fears versus incredible experiences of love and catharsis.

For the past couple of years, I have maintained a limited scope of personal reference. That scope began to expand again as the nature of my politics remained the same, while that of my community and my country took a wide turn in a different and far disparate direction.

At the Women's March in Portland this past spring, I joined in a huge gathering of like-minded people that painted a wide, colorful swath across humanity. With my daughter and husband by my side, we watched as downtown Portland was filled to bursting with the 100,000-plus peaceful throng, spilling out onto streets and sidewalks, pressed to expand by sheer numbers, shouting down from parking garages, apartments and office buildings. At one point my daughter asked why I wasn't chanting along with the rest of the crowd, and I answered honestly: "Little Sister, if I start to say anything, I'll cry. And if I start to cry, I'm afraid I won't stop."

This past Friday, my husband and I, in Portland for an appointment, stopped to eat lunch and take a moment to reflect at the Hollywood MAX Station, where just the week before a fellow Reed College alumnus, Taliesen Namkai-Meche, had lost his life. We walked along the up-sloping ramp, and I paused, here and there, to touch the chalk-drawn sentiments of strangers equally moved as I with feelings of sadness and loss. When I pulled my hand away, my fingers were smudged with the colorful chalk, just like those of the ones who had been there before me, and I felt an immediate sense of connection that brought tears to my eyes and peace to my heart.

Our quiet, impromptu moment turned into a crowd, and we

found ourselves present at a moment of silence that was shared across Portland, as all forms of public transportation halted, pulled over and quieted themselves in honor and remembrance of the events of the week before. What was supposed to be just a minute turned out the be much longer as no one dared break the silence, a welcome break from the rhetoric and invective, for fear of losing its power.

The next afternoon, we attended the ceremony in Mosier that called to reflect on the one-year anniversary of the oil train derailment and subsequent fire. Just yards away from the school where we gathered lies the area near Rock Creek that still reeks under the sun with the odor of oil and the reminder of the unmitigated greed and hubris that essentially guaranteed such a disaster, if not for us, at least somewhere along the line. We paused for a moment of silence, as the threatening sound of a train chugged along behind us.

Those of us who remember it well consider our glorious Gorge winds that were miraculously absent that afternoon. We are also reminded of that moment when our children clung to each other in fear and wept for their parents, just as parents, cut off from entering Mosier from every direction, feared desperately for their children. As we evacuated up valley, we wondered openly what we would come home to. The plumes of acrid black smoke turned the afternoon sun orange, mocking us as we ran away. Moments such as these are important to remember.

Sunday afternoon found us back in Portland under very different circumstances. I feared for my daughter's safety and opted not to bring her along, as the conflict of ideologies threatened to become violent by sheer proximity alone. Opposing voices stood separated by yellow crime tape (an omen?) and by a line of police and federal officers dressed in full riot gear.

My husband and I walked the perimeter, just to get a sense of the enormity of the moment. With our dogs in tow, we negotiated past the north side of the plaza along Chapman Park, which was filled five to 10 deep with members of the Antifa Movement, dressed in solid black from head to toe, faces obscured, standing in almost total silence, looking like trouble. At one point, we stepped off the curb to avoid the crowd, and I immediately felt equally intimidated by the doubling of the force sent to contain them. Loudspeakers threatened the crowd, ordering them to disperse. We inched our way back around, just in time to hear and feel from a mere block away the percussions from the "non-lethal" mortars fired by the police. As the crowd recoiled, my husband asked if we should leave, and I answered boldly and honestly: "No. We stand still. Right where we are."

In that moment of fear and unrest, a woman stopped and asked to pet our dogs, as hundreds had done so throughout the day. (We are blessed with two genuinely adorable corgis that tend to stop traffic and share a dose of "peace and Corgi love" as we call it, wherever we go.) She gripped my hand after sharing a hug, and with an air of sadness and desperation asked, "I've been doing this sort of thing since the '60s. Why are we still doing this?" Caught off guard, I answered honestly: "I don't know …"

Moments later, a little boy sank unexpectedly to the curb on his knees in front of us, enraptured by our dogs. He engaged us with a boldly cheerful, eager demeanor, markedly different from the sentiment of the crowd surrounding us on every side. He gave me a hug that carried with it the strength of an open mind and a trusting heart. In that moment, I wanted to find the woman from before and reassure her in all honesty: "Here, Ma'am. Right here. This little boy. See the light in his eyes. This is why we do this."

Amy's article can be found online at https://bit.ly/3E5uLeI.

ACKNOWLEDGEMENTS

Since this wasn't an intentional book in the usual sense, and since the bulk of it comes from Facebook posts presented as-written, it has been less of a group effort than would typically be the case. The intimate, personal, and journal-like nature of the content likely contributes to that also, since there's no single, linear narrative for anyone else to help me craft. Nonetheless, I could not have done this on my own.

The Portland Re-evaluation Counseling community provided me with perspective and tools for a lifetime of healing, including a framework for understanding and expressing my feelings, all of which made it possible for me both to write the Facebook posts that became this book, and to process my grief the way I did.

It took a lot to overcome my reticence to add "yet another book about death" to the world. Much of the required push came from the daily flow of people appreciating the honesty or rawness or insights they drew from my posts. Though I can't list all those people, I can highlight some. Juliana Tobón was the first to encourage me to keep going on Facebook, when I was starting to feel self-conscious that I was still "going on" about my grief after most people would've stopped. Judy and Johan Maurer were the first to suggest the potential usefulness of a book version of what I was writing on Facebook. Ramona Mittelstadt has been perhaps my most vocal, ardent, and steadfast fan from the outset. A random encounter with Brenna Campbell, in which she teared up while describing how much what I was writing meant to her, convinced me more than anything else that this book was a good idea.

My dad, Bob Worsley, and my sister, Honor Doherty, enthusiastically supported the idea. Honor went an enormous leap further in offering to publish it—and to donate the effort involved out of a strong belief in and support for this project. She and her lead editor and designer, Leslie F. Peters of Together Editing & Design, provided a much smoother and more professional experience than I'd ever have had trying to publish this myself.

About the Author

John R. Worsley wants to identify as a screenwriter, but as with his IT career, finds himself collecting multiple hats along the way. He has always loved playing with words, and remembers at the age of four referring to his elbow as his "ell bone" — because his arm was shaped like the letter L. Growing up, he read constantly (200 books one summer for a library contest), engaged in creative word usement with his siblings (many nouns were verbed), and actually enjoyed writing essays in school.

In high school he began to see himself as a writer, thanks to a creative writing class — in which he wrote his first story by imagining it as a movie — and teacher encouragement. In college, he tried to become a geophysicist, but somehow ended up with a job writing press releases and (perhaps the acme of word and language geekery) a B.A. in linguistics, after which he stumbled into IT. Even there, he still found himself crafting with words as a technical writer.

Along the way, he dabbled with short poetry, flash fiction, short stories, a novelette, and a novel, and started a non-fiction book on sustainability. Then in 2007, he discovered and fell in love with screenwriting, which became the focus of his writing life. ... Well, except for the long poem he published in 2016. And the memoir he ghostwrote in 2017. And the graphic novel project he started in 2019. And that playwriting class. And now this non-fiction book.

Made in the USA
Monee, IL
27 July 2022